The Not-So-Evil Stepmother in the Most Magical Place on Earth

Planning Your Walt Disney World Family Vacation

Trisha Daab

Theme Park Press
www.ThemeParkPress.com

Editor: Bob McLain
Layout: Artisanal Text
Cover Art: Samantha Carol Stadlman, MAAT, LPC

ISBN 979-8-89609-148-6
Printed in the United States of America

Theme Park Press | **www.ThemeParkPress.com**
Address queries to ben@themeparkpress.com

This book is dedicated to my grandma, the first person to take me to Disney; the one who taught me to wear heels because they "make your legs look longer;" and the one who knew how important it is to marry your best friend.

Contents

Introduction

Wishes, Fantasy & French Food:
10 Years of Walt Disney World Magic

I love a Disney vacation. There is nothing that makes me forget all the stress and anxiety of daily life like a Disney vacation. When you are there, you are in this bubble where the most stressful thing is making it to your FP+ (FastPass) or dinner reservation on time, and where the most important decision is whether to ride Expedition Everest again when the stand-by line is only 30 minutes.

One of the best parts of the Disney vacation for me is the planning stage. Then I love sitting back and watching as my family enjoys the results of my plans. And my family is big, varies in age, and loves to eat! My husband, Joe, and I have a blended family. A yours, mine, and ours. I am the bonus mom of three: Nate, Maggie, and Annie (the yours) from Joe's previous marriage. Joe is the bonus dad of Austin (the mine) from my previous marriage, and together we have Oliver (the ours.) Throw in my mom and dad, and a couple of the older kids' significant others, and the Evil Stepmother (or Bonus Mom as we call it in our house) is planning a vacation for 11, and it's a blast.

The Not-So-Evil Stepmother in the Most Magical Place on Earth is divided into four Disney Experiences with multiple chapters within each experience. Sprinkled throughout the experiences, like pixie dust, are tips for having the most magical Disney vacation. Also included are the Stepmom's Seven Disney Secrets. You can find these at the end of each experience. These secrets will help you plan your Disney vacation, select the Disney hotel where you will rest your weary head and the Disney restaurants where you will fill your empty stomachs, decide what to reserve and pack, and get your crew excited for the adventures to come. The tips and secrets are based on our family's experiences and the fun of planning for a couple, a trio, a wedding for eight, and a 10-year anniversary trip for 11.

At the beginning of each experience, you'll find stories of our trips to Disney World. You'll hear from a clan of 11—with kids ages 7–26, plus grandparents—about their favorite moments, meals, and rides from our most recent trip to celebrate our 10-year wedding anniversary! You'll experience the beauty of a "post-Thanksgiving but before Christmas crowds" trip. You'll find out what it's like to have a Disney wedding, and you'll learn about what makes Disney magical at every age. And you'll share in one of our favorite parts of any trip—the food—as you travel Walt Disney World with our blended family of food lovers, magically munching from Jiko and the Epcot Food & Wine Festival to Be Our Guest and Coca-Cola's Club Cool.

Before every trip I would always seek out new and different books to read to get me excited. Most of the time I wasn't looking for a planning guide but just something that could whisk me away and remind me of all the fun to come. My hope is that reading this book is akin to having a coffee and a chat with a clever friend who is telling you about her Disney trips while helping you plan your own. This is a book to get you excited for your next trip. Or to get a little Disney fix between trips. Maybe to find a new food you want to try on your next trip. Or to experience Disney through a different set of eyes.

Come along with us and experience the Most Magical Place on Earth, not-so-evil stepmother style.

Experience 2005: Disney for 8

She's gonna be a nice stepmother. She's gonna take you to school tomorrow, just you and her, for some grown-up girl-bonding time.

—Robert Philip, the dad in Disney's *Enchanted*

CHAPTER ONE
Four Parks and a Beach Club

"We should get married. We want to go to Disney. What if we do both? What, get married at Disney? We're going to Disney World? All of us?!"

This was the beginning of the next stage of our becoming a family—an eventual "yours, mine, and ours" – and me becoming a not-so-evil stepmother. I did a lot of planning for this trip, hitting the library for guidebooks, Amazon for more guidebooks, and doing a ton of online research, though there were far fewer sources for Disney theme park information back in those days. My research included creating a rough day-by-day schedule so I could make dining reservations and determine the necessity for the Park Hopper, which we purchased but didn't use. I also figured out all the attractions we wanted to see at each park so I could then determine which parks we needed to visit more than once. My future stepchildren regularly picked on me for the amount of planning I did, but today they tell me how much they appreciate it.

Cast

At this stage we were just a yours and mine (the ours was to come later). So, starting from our wisest and closest in age to Walt:

- Dad (Bob), also known as Grandpa Bob, the Bobarazzi (because he is always behind the camera), Bobert, father of the bride, and for me, Bonus Dad. It was Bob's commitment to photography that made it possible for all of us to look back and 10 years later remember our favorite moments from the trip. This was his third trip to Disney World.

- Mom (Debbie), also known as Grandma Dubbie, mother of the bride and, jokingly, Mumsy. The thrill-seeker of the group, she also had the best and most healthy snacks. This was her fourth trip to Disney World.

- Joe, also known as Dad and Sonny Boy (from my mom). Joe was the genius who suggested having our wedding on the second day of the trip so I wouldn't be freaking out the whole week. This was his fourth trip to Disney World.

- Me, also known as Mom, Sis (from my mom), Trish, and the future evil stepmother (from my bonus kids Annie, Maggie and Nate). This was my fifth trip to Disney World (and my second one as an adult).

- Nate, 16 years old and the subject of an inordinate number of Bob's photos, as Nate had to do a presentation on his trip for French class. This was his second trip to Disney World.

- Maggie, also known as Mags, 13 years old, an avid writer (which came in very handy for this book), and most committed student of the group; she even stayed in the hotel one day to get her homework done. This was her second trip to Disney World.

- Annie, also known as Ann, eight years old and in constant search of Tigger. Annie was far less worried about her schoolwork. This was her second trip to Disney (and the first she remembered).

- Austin, five years old and not at all worried about his schoolwork. Austin had been to Disney World earlier this year and several other times as well (because his dad's parents had a timeshare in Orlando). This was his fourth trip to Disney World.

- Also with us just for the wedding and the following day was my best friend, Becky. We have been friends since we were in diapers and she is like part of the family. My parents know her, she loves Joe. and Becky is is like a young, quirky, fun aunt for all the kids.

Itinerary

- *Day 1.* We arrived on an early flight Sunday, November 27, 2005, and headed straight to the Magic Kingdom for dinner at Crystal Palace.

- *Day 2.* Epcot. Lunch at Les Chefs de France, dinner at Jiko.

- *Day 3.* Disney-MGM (now Hollywood) Studios. Brunch at 50's Prime Time Cafe, late lunch Sci-Fi Dine-In Theater, and Fantasmic! Dinner Package at Mama Melrose.

- *Day 4.* Epcot. Breakfast in room, dinner at Restaurant Marrakesh.

- *Day 5.* Animal Kingdom. Character breakfast at Restaurantosaurus.

- *Day 6.* Magic Kingdom. Late lunch at Cinderella's Royal Table, then Mickey's Very Merry Christmas Party.

- *Day 7.* Downtown Disney. Shopping, shopping, more shopping.

- *Day 8.* We pack all the stuff we bought while shopping, shopping, and more shopping, and fly home.

The Beach Club

"Don't stay at the BoardWalk. The hotel is huge and you can have an almost mile walk just to get to your room. I'd try Beach Club," advisded a work colleague. (I wish she had been around when I booked Kidani Village for our 2015 trip, but more on that later.) So Beach Club Villas it was. And we were in luck, as they had a 2-bedroom villa available which fit our party of six perfectly. My folks stayed at Coronado Springs so they could easily have a break from our crowd. It's the perfect resort for them, with its scenic walks, beautiful flowers, and affordable breakfast buffet. But for this trip, Beach Club Villas was pretty close to perfect for us.

Day 1

I try to schedule our flights for as early as possible. If all goes well at the airport, you reach Orlando with at least half a day to hit a park. Never rely or plan anything important for that first day because it almost ensures your flight will be delayed. We live in Chicago and were traveling in winter so the likelihood of delays was high. With FastPass and the cancellation fees for Disney dining reservations, make sure you don't schedule any high-priority destinations on your travel day. This can also help reduce your stress if something does go wrong on your travels that affects your plans for the parks.

We were lucky. All went well and we were in the Magic Kingdom a bit tired after being up at 3 a.m., but way too excited to nap. Back then, Disney didn't charge for skipped dining reservations, so I had scheduled a character dinner at Crystal Palace. "Buffets are the best," was Nate's opinion of Crystal Palace. The restaurant has a pretty extensive buffet, with many tasty options. There is even an ice cream bar, which was a huge hit with the kids. "Tigger, Pooh, and Tigger!" Annie cried. Her love of Tigger was one of the reasons we booked Crystal Palace on the first day, to get the trip off to a good start for Annie. She was excited to see her favorite character and gave him a ton of hugs, giving us many sweet photo opportunities.

One of the magical moments of any Disney trip is when your kids first spot the characters. You see them walking around the restaurant and the anticipation builds as they get closer and closer to your table. That is what is great about character meals and having one early in your trip. You see the character coming and have time to prepare rather than chasing after your kid while scrambling to pull out your camera. If there is a character you really want to see, and there is a character meal that features them, do that. Not only does it ensure you will get to see the character, you won't have long waits in line to fill your autograph book.

Winter in Orlando can be surprisingly chilly. We were lucky that at the end of our first night it was still warm once the sun went down. It was on this night that Annie, Maggie, Austin, Joe, and I decided to hit the pool. Austin's favorite part of our Beach Club room was that he could not only see the pool from our room, we could basically almost jump to it from our patio and had the place to ourselves. Often the pools at the resorts are very crowded and high energy, and unless you are chasing after your kids on the slides, you don't see them much.

The Beach Club Villas pool was just a pool with a set of deck chairs surrounding it. The closest thing to a slide was the rail, which Austin and Annie both slid down. I preferred it to the much busier, themed Yacht/Beach Club pool. That pool felt very Disney, with the sand-bottom and pirate ship slide, and is considered by many to be one of the best resort pools, but the close proximity of the Beach Club Villa pool and its relative seclusion made it feel almost like it was our own.

Joe, the kids, and I were also together the whole time, splashing, talking, and laughing with each other. We hit the big pool one day, though it was a bit chilly when we weren't in the water. For the rest of the trip, it was typically in the mid-70s during the day, but the evenings were very cool. It was good we did the pool when we did.

> **TIP!** Dress in layers no matter what time of year you are at Disney. Even when it's sweltering hot and you are sticky the second you walk outside, Floridians love their air conditioning. Many of the attractions are frigid. You may want to don a light sweater before you enter the castle at Be Our Guest or zip up your hoodie before the Great Movie Ride.

CHAPTER TWO
The Evil Stepmother's Disney Wedding

Day 2

Day two dawned cloudy with a steady drizzle. It was warm and Florida humid. "We may need to move the location of the ceremony because of the weather," said our Disney wedding planner. "We have another great location. It's a bit less private but a beautiful place for the ceremony." This is where Joe's calmness and go-with-the-flow-attitude came in very handy. He convinced me all would still be wonderful and that we should go with our original plan of hanging in Epcot before the wedding.

In less than 10 minutes we were posing in a phone booth in the UK pavilion. That was the best part of the Beach Club: a short walk to World Showcase. Epcot is our favorite park and World Showcase is the highlight for us.

We started our Epcot experience with one of the best parts of any vacation, delicious food, and had lunch at Le Chefs de France in the France pavilion. We had a lovely young man from France as our "garçon" and were lucky to sit in the front sunroom, where we had a 180-degree view of the fountain and square in the main part of the France pavilion. The sunroom has a very French bistro style, with a creamy white, ornate ceiling, reminiscent of a few of the bistros Joe and I had visited in France. All the kids really loved this meal. This was the first time we tried the lobster bisque, which has brought us back to Le Chefs many times over the years. We also had a Margherita-style pizza with a tangy tomato sauce, fresh basil, and salty, stringy cheese on a European-style, super-thin, cracker-like crust. I know how much everyone loved this meal because we have photographic evidence of the smiles, bites, and even Annie looking longingly at Nate biting into his pizza.

After touring the World Showcase for a few hours, it was time to shop. A few weeks before the wedding, my future bonus son, Nate, told me, "As soon as you and my Dad say 'I do,' you're going to become a 'yonko mother' (a mythical evil creature from Nate's imagination). Your eyes are going to glow red, your hair will go crazy, and you will start floating." This became the running joke leading up to the trip. My transformation was captured in a photo of me wearing Figment ears with Stitch paws using my evil stepmotherness to terrorize my soon-to-be stepdaughter, Annie.

In the early afternoon, the girls and I hit the salon at the Beach Club to get our hair done. The ladies there were friendly, good at engaging with a tween, and did a beautiful job creating three gorgeous up-dos for Annie, Maggie, and me. This was a suggestion from our wedding planner. Our wedding was called an Intimate Ceremony (similar to the Escape Collection they have now). For about $3600 we had a unique, kid-friendly, quick ceremony for 13 people. The standard package included the ceremony space, officiant, cake, champagne toast, live music, portrait style photographer, photo album, flowers, marriage certificate, special gift, transportation, and a planner.

The ceremony space was originally the Rose Gazebo in the center courtyard of the Yacht Club. This is a quiet and intimate space, far less public than some of the other spaces we considered, including the gazebo between the Boardwalk and Beach Club. With the weather, the Rose Gazebo wasn't possible because you have to walk outdoors for a bit to get there.

When we chose to get married at Disney and selected the affordable Intimate Ceremony, we got a lot of flack from friends and family who couldn't come because of the 13-person maximum allowed. The funny part was we ended up having our ceremony at a gazebo space near the main pool of both hotels. So, not only was our family present in the gazebo space, but we also had about 50 random strangers cheering us on as they hung out by the pool, walked by on their way into the hotel, or departed or arrived on the Friendship boats. All of our friends and family could have easily seen us get married, but instead it was groups of park-goers in their fanny packs and tennis shoes. Disney did block off a few small areas so that my father was able to walk me down the aisle, a pretty brick walkway into the gazebo, and we almost didn't notice all the strangers looking on. It wasn't until the very end—during our kiss—that we heard the applause and realized our audience had swelled to far over the 13-person limit.

Our officiant was a high-energy, charismatic man named Jack Day. I think every conversation we had on the phone he was in his car. The most memorable chat was when he asked, "What would you like me to be wearing? I can do the formal robes, but I also have this great suit. And I can wear a tie that will go with the colors of your ceremony." This is my kind of wedding officiant. Jack not only had a variety of wardrobe options, he also had a few different ceremonies he could perform and you picked the one that fit you best.

With Jack in our Intimate Ceremony cast of characters was our Disney wedding planner. When we moved the day of our ceremony from the end of the trip to the beginning, we learned that the planner they assign is based on the day and time of the wedding. We had a wonderful woman named Marie for the majority of the planning. She was receptive, understanding, and responsive to my type-A planning personality. She helped me customize the package to our needs and offered great suggestions on the location and when it was worth paying extra.

"You are not going to be able to enjoy yourself. You're going to be thinking about the wedding and all the plans the whole trip. We should do it earlier in the week," said my future husband, knowing me quite well. Originally, I had scheduled the wedding for a day later in the week. But after grudgingly admitting Joe was right, I moved it to Monday, our second day at Disney. This meant losing Marie and having a new planner who was not as knowledgeable, friendly, or detail-oriented, which was demonstrated before and after the ceremony when we received multiple letters and packages addressed to Brandon and Trisha Daab. Not sure who Brandon is, but he was no Joe. Thankfully, it was Joe's name she got wrong, because he was much more understanding of the mistake than I would have been.

The planner also attends the ceremony, meeting you near your location with the flowers and photographers and escorting you to your final destination. The best part is they help you with dining reservations. With a party of nine, these can be tricky. On the day of our wedding our new planner fell ill, which was honestly not a huge loss, especially since it was Marie who replaced her! The planner stays the entire ceremony and even handles the daunting marriage license paperwork. This keeps you from having to spend at least half a day of your vacation running to a Florida courthouse. You have to love Disney and their power to have the rules changed for them.

On the wedding day, the planner has a number of jobs including helping the men in your life put on boutonnieres. In 2005 Austin could not stand still (10 year later he still doesn't unless it involves playing Madden Mobile on his iPhone), and Marie had the fun task of trying to stick a restless five-year-old with a needle and not draw blood. The fact that she did it, and he had a smile on his face the whole time, is a testament to her abilities. The girls had flowers they carried that looked like wands with pixie dust and ribbons, which they loved, and my mom had a corsage. The flowers were beautiful bright blue and light purple hydrangeas. So much of what Disney does well is the small details that truly matter. A crowd favorite was the cream-colored satin ribbon in my bouquet that was held on by a hidden Mickey in pearls.

We opted for the live music and had a violinist who happily played the series of Cole Porter songs we'd requested in place of the standard *Pachelbel's Canon*. Another upgrade that we would recommend whole-heartily is adding a "photo-journalist" to document the event. At the time, this upgrade cost us around $600 and included one additional photo album. It was money well spent. When I booked I thought we would be having the photo-journalist in place of the portrait photographer. It wasn't until we walked into the Yacht Club as a family and had our red carpet moment, being temporarily blinded as we were bombarded with a series of lights and flashes from two photographers and the videographer, that I realized upgrading meant we would have both. Once the spots in our vision went away, we met the whole team capturing our big moment.

The two photographers played off each other really well, and often times the photo-journalist would be capturing the hilarity that was trying to wrangle all nine of us and getting us to pose nicely. That is not the Daab way. We much prefer to pose dramatically or in interesting ways. My father, Bob, calls it Daab style. One of my favorite wedding photos is all of us in our wedding finery on a beautiful grand staircase tastefully decorated for the holidays in the Yacht Club. Austin is doing a little dance with his mouth hanging open, Nate is holding his knee up and making a "karate man" face, with Annie next to him doing a similar pose, Maggie is singing into her bouquet, Joe's arms are spread wide like the master of the wackiness and I am looking at him and giving him a smile that says, "Yep, this was totally worth it. I love this family." Even my mom is getting in on the action, saying, "Well, if you can't get them to pose, give up and we'll just join them." Bob is standing there with a huge grin and sympathizing with the photographers.

> **TIP!** If you are having a Disney wedding, make good friends with your photographer. Find out which one will be doing the selects for your photo album afterward. Be a happy photo subject, be friendly, make them laugh, cooperate, and call them after your wedding. This way you get more say on which photos make it into your album, and you don't end up with a photo of you, your spouse, and your Cinderella and Prince Charming watches. (Or maybe that's your thing and you can make sure you get more than one!)

Picking the photos that will go in your Disney wedding album is very important. Nowadays, with digital photos, this may all have changed, but at the time, between our two albums, we only got 23 of the hundreds of photos the guys took. If you wanted to receive a disc with the photos it was pretty pricey. Thankfully, the photo-journalist remembered us and had a great time with our wacky group and let me choose the photos I wanted in the album.

As is true with most things Disney, they had a standard set included in the package: a professional photo of Joe and me with a Cinderella-themed certificate from a vice president at Disney, congratulating us on our wedding. It's a nice piece in a beautiful folder. The certificate is accompanied by "a gift from Cinderella and Prince Charming to commemorate your special day," presented by the planner. Now, we are Disney fans, but not the kind who wear watches with the castle on them. They are very nice watches and the eBay buyer who paid $150 for them is probably very happy. The looks on our faces while holding our new Disney gifts of "aren't these great. What the hell are we going to do with this?" did make for a funny photo—but with only 23 options, it wasn't at the top of my list.

Huge thanks to our Disney photographer for understanding and having a laugh with me when I begged him not to include that pic. The upgrade to the videographer included a VHS of the ceremony. Yes, a VHS. It's now 2016 and we don't even have a way we can watch our wedding. I think we watched it once and decided we never needed to watch it again. Some people are meant for screen, I definitely am not. But it was worth having because the kids thought it was pretty cool and it was fun to see their reactions that we missed while there.

"What's with all the love stuff?" This was the question Austin asked as we were nearing the end of the ceremony. Throughout the ceremony, Austin had been slowly picking off the flowers on his boutonniere petal by petal. As we neared the end, he slowly slid down one of the columns he was leaning against and was squatting down with a circle of petals around his feet. The photographer caught the moment when Austin asked the question and we all looked at him with his chin in his hands surround by all his blue and purple petals and laughed. One of my dad's pics of the day is of me, in my wedding dress, holding Austin's suit jacket with what looks like a stick attached with a beautiful pearl pin. Austin doesn't remember any of this, but the older kids all do. Nate even remembers telling him, "Umm, it's a wedding, dude. There's love stuff."

Bringing together a family with children ages 5 to 16 doesn't happen everyday, so there weren't any passages or sets of vows that really encompassed all we wanted to say. There was a paragraph that we included for Jack to say that talked about coming together and forming a new family. Joe and I also really wanted the kids to know how important a role they had played in getting us to this point, so we wrote our own vows. As we learned at our anniversary dinner during our 2015 trip, the fact that we had written our vows was memorable to Nate—that and Joe crying tears of joy. Ten years later, Nate said it was the first time he really knew what true love was.

After the ceremony, Disney provides a Fairytale Cuvee champagne toast. We upgraded and added a bottle of sparkling apple cider, which went over like gangbusters with the kids. We have a great photo of the four of them toasting Joe and I, and they all had fun pretending they were drinking actual champagne. That was a really good thing because the cake did not impress. It was beautiful, piled high with white frosting that looked like clouds with a porcelain castle resting on top. Annie had been eyeing the cake the entire ceremony and was so excited to take the first bite. Sadly, it was a lot prettier than it tasted. The frosting was lush and silky and tasted like they just whipped butter without any sugar. It was a huge disappointment, but at least it looked good.

Thankfully, we were having a delicious and unique dinner at Jiko at the Animal Kingdom Lodge after the ceremony. This was another instance where having a wedding planner proved invaluable because she arranged our much-needed transportation to the Animal Kingdom Lodge. To this day, transportation between resorts at Disney is tricky and often requires taking a bus to a park and then taking another bus to your desired resort. Our planner arranged for two limos to take us to Jiko and then back to our resort and my parents back to theirs. The kids all loved the limo ride; it made it into that day's journal entry for both Maggie and Austin.

Jiko is an experience. It is one of the top fine-dining restaurants in all of Disney World. The folks at Jiko knew this was a big day for us and were excited to have us. They even sent over a bottle of champagne. The staff at Jiko is from all over the world (you may even have someone from Africa) and very knowledgeable about the food. One of our servers was amazed by the size of our family and worked hard to understand how we were all related. The food was delicious and we got the kids to try new things, including an appetizer called the Taste of Africa. The flavors and dishes are authentic and true to what you would have if in South Africa. One thing to try when at Disney is to give your kids new experiences and exposure to new flavors and Jiko is a delicious way to do it.

Our Disney wedding was everything we had hoped, filled with tasty food, love, family, and Disney magic. Austin summed it up best in his trip journal entry: "We did get married."

CHAPTER THREE
Sci Fi, Belly Dancers, and Soarin'

Day 3

We are married! We've had a day of dressing-up, a tasty meal at Jiko, and even a bit of time at Epcot. Day three is the day of food, Fantasmic!, and lights at Hollywood Studios. We knew we wanted to eat at Sci-Fi Dine-In Theater as that was on Nate's list and I also wanted to try the 50's Prime Time Cafe. Also on the list was the Fantasmic! dinner package at Mama Melrose. This was really the day of too much food, but meals are my favorite part of our Disney trips because everyone is together, we talk about what we have seen and the magic to come, and it's a time for family, with minimal distractions.

But three sit-down meals in one day is just too many.

The day started with a super early lunch at the 50's Prime Time Cafe where the peanut-butter-and-jelly shakes were a highlight. This was also the first time on Tower of Terror for Austin, Annie, Bob, Joe, Nate, Mags, and Becky. My mom and I had been on a previous trip and knew how awesome it was. The anticipation of slowly riding through the hotel and seeing the black-and-white figures beckoning you, the strobe lights, and then the complete darkness before the first drop is a huge and fun adrenaline rush. The best part is not knowing when and how far the next drop will be. This ride became a favorite of many in our group. Rock 'n' Roller Coaster was also on the list. My mom is always the most excited to hit the thrill rides. Even Dad gave this one a try, though won't be riding it again.

Lunch was very late at the Sci-Fi Dine-In Theater. Sci-Fi is one of our favorite restaurants because it is so fun to sit in old cars and watch the trailers for old movies, like *Attack of the 50-Foot Woman*. The layout of the restaurant is like an old 1950's drive-in theatre. It is well themed, down to the walls looking like a neighborhood. I always request to sit in the cars and it's a nice time to sit and relax where the kids still feel like they are doing something cool. Sci-Fi serves a great burger and fries. It can be a bit pricey, but with the limited number of attractions at Hollywood Studios, eating at Sci-Fi helps to feel like it's worth the price of admission.

The Honey I Shrunk the Kids playground gave the adults a chance to sit and digest while the kids ran around. It's a fun space where everything from Kodak film cases to ants are oversized. This is one of those times to just sit and let the kids enjoy some Disney magic. Rides are a blast, the shows are amazing, but sometimes kids just want to climb, run, and scream. This space is perfect for those activities.

Another "to do" between rides and shows is shopping. From the Star Wars store to the shops along the boulevards, you can pick up unique merchandise at Hollywood Studios. Keystone Clothiers is one of our favorite stores as they carry nice clothing and jewelry. Joe and I fall into the camp of folks who are not the "large Goofy on a t-shirt" type, and we have always been able to find additions to our wardrobe at this shop. We also tried on many different Mickey ears, from the bride-and-groom version to those with a holiday theme. Becky was DisneyBounding (dressing up as a modern version of your favorite Disney character) before it was even a thing and there is a great photo of her in a cute rose-colored-with-white-polka-dots t-shirt with an adorable pair of holiday Minnie ears. Becky has always been a trendsetter.

The food portion of our day at MGM ended with dinner at Mama Melrose. Now this is probably a tasty and delicious place, but most of us were still full of burgers and shakes from Sci-Fi. The Fantasmic! dinner package has a pre-set menu where you choose an appetizer, entree, dessert, and drink. Maggie, who today is gluten-free, said, "I remember that pasta. Disney with gluten was just tastier." Maggie found gluten-free Disney in 2015 to still be tasty—just with less pasta.

Fantasmic! is the park's nighttime show, a spectacle of fireworks, lights, music, and many of everyone's favorite Disney characters live and in person. The combination of the famous Disney couples on boats, the projections on the water, and cheering on Mickey to defeat a gigantic snake make Fantasmic! a show not to be missed. From a five-year-old who had seen the show three times to Grandpa's first experience, everyone was on the edge of their cement bleachers (seats are a bit of a stretch, but the seating is plenty comfortable for the relatively short time you are there).

Is the Fantasmic! dinner package worth it? If you don't have a full docket of Hollywood Studios' rides using up your FP+ or can visit the park more than once on your trip, try to get a FP+ on the day you are at Hollywood Studios. If you're there during the busy times of Thanksgiving and Christmas, spring break, the summer months, or Star Wars weekends, go with the dinner package.

Day 4

For most of the trip we ate breakfast in the room. This is a great way to save money and it gives the kids a chance to relax before the day starts. It is also helpful when you have a big group and the time it takes to get ready varies.

A small group of us started the day on Mission: SPACE, including thrill-seeker Grandma Debbie. One thing not to miss at Epcot is Club Cool. It's a bit tucked away before you get to the Land pavilion near Innoventions West. This was another of those moments that most of the kids still remember. At Club Cool you can sample different brands of Coke from around the world and many of the flavors can be quite surprising. During our 2015 visit, we once again visited Club Cool and found it is no longer a hidden gem. The place was packed. Nate was amazed by the flavors he remembered from ten years earlier.

As an early Christmas present for my parents, we got them the Segway tour of Epcot. My dad loved getting to ride a Segway, which was still pretty new technology at the time. My mom is a flower fan and she loved learning about all the work done by the landscapers and decorators to make Epcot a showcase for the beauty of the holidays around the world. Which brings up an important point: sometimes to truly enjoy a Disney vacation with a large group, you have to split up. That's hard for me to do because I am all about the family being together on our vacations, but this was a nice chance for my parents to have time to themselves and have a "date" during the trip. They returned the favor a few nights later when they took the kids out while Joe and I had a tasty dinner at the France pavilion in Epcot.

We were lucky to experience Soarin' in its first year. This was the year of the Happiest Celebration on Earth, and Disney World had imported a number of attractions from different parks around the world. I remember folks talking about Soarin' and how an attraction about California would probably not be that popular. Well, in the three times I have been at Epcot since the arrival of Soarin' in 2005, it has been one of the longest lines and hardest to obtain FastPasses. It still delights every time. Our whole crew had no idea what to expect.

To board Soarin' you enter a dark room with rows of "paragliders" dangling from the ceiling. The paragliders are huge and our whole group fit in the seats on just one of the three rows. You buckle yourself in and then the magic starts. The paragliders rise high into the air and move forward so you are dangling in front of a huge screen. The music starts and suddenly you are transported to a bird's-eye view of California. Through a combination of blowing wind, scents in the air, your feet dangling down, and the paraglider swooping up, down, left, and right, you feel like a bird flying through the air over well-known California landmarks. Our whole crew exclaimed over the experience of smelling the oranges and pine trees, swooping dangerously close to the snow skiers and surfers, and hovering above Disneyland with the castle and fireworks in view. Soarin' is an attraction not to be missed. (Now, of course, you soar not over California, but around the world.)

Test Track is one of those rides that people either love or hate. Back in 2005, it was a ride in a gray open-topped car. While waiting in line you can see different tests that the vehicles go through. As you get closer to the boarding area, there are graphics on the wall of the test dummies. The fun part was there were dummies that almost perfectly fit Annie, Austin, Nate, Maggie, Joe, and I. There were no superhero sedans back in the day, so we climbed into our gray test vehicle and started the ride.

One of the first stops was to test the car in the elements. The car pulled into a room that looked like a vault with large red heaters all around. It felt like standing on the blacktop during a hot Florida day, just not as humid or drippy. Then it was extreme cold, which was like any indoor Florida restaurant. The car continued weaving its way through the tests and then stopped outside a set of double doors and the countdown began. At "1," the car is launched outdoors, the speedometer quickly rising as it flies around tight turns before doing a brake test to slow it down. At some point during the acceleration test, Disney snaps a pic of your hair whipping around your face, and in the case of Maggie, death-gripping the handlebar screaming at the top of her lungs. It's not a thrill ride on par with the dropping-to-your-doom fear of Tower of Terror or the where-am-I-going darkness of Space Mountain, but it's a lot of fun.

For most of our group, the best part of Epcot is wandering around World Showcase. The shops at World Showcase provide a lot of material for dressing up and pretending to be different characters. From the gigantic sombreros in the Mexico pavilion to berets in France to Viking hats in Norway, we have many photos of Nate becoming a local character in his uniquely animated way. One of our favorite photos from this trip came from one of the shops. We were hanging out in Norway when Austin asked, "Can I buy that?" holding a sword and wearing one of the Viking helmets. As we contemplated where to fit the sword in our luggage, Austin proceeded to engage in battle with a large man, also in a Viking helmet, but this one had the long blonde pigtail braids.

What we especially love about the World Showcase is that in addition to traveling around the world, you can also taste your way around the world. The quick-service restaurants all have country-specific tasty treats and the sit-down restaurants have some of the best theming in all of Disney World. San Angel Inn in the Mexico pavilion is set in twilight and located right on the water. It is quite romantic. Joe and I can say from experience that Les Chefs de France is pretty close to being in France, minus the cigarette smoke and small dogs. All it needs is outdoor seating and it will really feel like a Parisian cafe.

Despite all the amazing tastes and delicious desserts Annie begged Joe, "Can I just have a chocolate-chip cookie?"

This was the day we all tried something new when we visited Restaurant Marrakesh in Morocco. Disney describes it as transporting you to the heart of Morocco and this restaurant is definitely a hidden gem, one of the best-themed, most authentic World Showcase restaurants most people have never been to. Restaurant Marrakesh is tucked far back in the Morocco pavilion. You enter through an ornately decorated lobby area, then a host takes you into a large, ballroom-like dining area with soaring ceilings and tiled pillars where you are greeted by live musicians playing authentic Moroccan music. And the smells. Meats roasting in cinnamon and spices, rice flavored with curry and dried fruits, and the sweet aroma of phyllo dough mixed with powdered sugar and almonds. This is not the tourist version of Moroccan food.

Adding to the ambience was the beautiful, talented, and exotic-looking belly dancer. Watching Austin watching the belly dancer was the real highlight. We were on one side of the dining area, and the belly dancer was in the middle or on the other side. Austin was initially sitting with his back to her, but upon discovering her presence and dancing ability he sat enthralled with his back turned to us during her entire performance. He kept eating, though, not once turning around but just reaching back to grab bites from his sultan sampler, so as not to miss a moment of the belly dancer. "Where did she go?" he asked as soon as she was done and left the room. "I have to go to the bathroom." I had to then follow him as he walked around looking for the belly dancer.

This was another bonding moment for the whole family because all the older kids gave their little brother a hard time and Nate and Maggie gave us a look that said, "Have fun with that in the future!" Learning that your five-year-old loves belly dancing and your new family loves cinnamon-spiced meat—just another magical day at Epcot.

After having our fill of chicken kebabs, roast lamb meshoui, beef brewat (beef pastries sprinkled with cinnamon and powdered sugar), and bastilla (crispy leaves of pastry with toasted almonds, cinnamon, and powdered sugar), we were ready to see Illuminations, Epcot's nighttime fireworks extravaganza. Or so we thought. All of us were dressed in pants and long-sleeve shirts or light jackets, but that was still not enough to keep us warm during Illuminations. Nearly every guest at a Disney park has begrudgingly handed over $20.00 for ponchos, only to have the rain stop 10 minutes later. We had done that just the day before at Disney-MGM Studios. But blankets? In Florida? Yep. It can get pretty chilly in the winter, especially around the lagoon. So, the blankets we procured from the Mexico pavilion appear in most of the photos from that evening.

Day 5

Day five started off cool but nothing compared to the previous evening. We donned our light layers and headed to Animal Kingdom for a character breakfast at Restaurantosaurus. This was our first Mickey waffle of the trip. Those little Mickey-shaped nuggets of goodness are a must for any Disney vacation. If you hit the buffet at just the right time, you can get one piping hot from the waffle iron. It will be crispy on the outside and moist on the inside. Add a dollop of fluffy whipped cream with crunchy bacon, that just happens to get a bit of maple syrup on it, and it's the perfect sweet/savory breakfast. This buffet breakfast (which has since been moved to Tusker House) is a great way to see the Fab Five (Mickey, Minnie, Donald, Pluto, and Goofy—plus Daisy, who isn't technically part of the Fab Five; maybe she's the Yoko Ono of the group). It's busy, but it's not as difficult to get a reservation here as it is at Chef Mickey's, another popular Fab Five character breakfast spot.

After breakfast we hit every part of the Animal Kingdom. During our adventure in DinoLand USA, I once again made a complete fool of myself in the photo on the DINOSAUR ride. Even though I know when that huge red T-Rex is going to come barreling out of the trees, it scares the crap out of me every time. This trip there is a photo of me screaming my head off while Austin sits calmly next to me. Nate's favorite attraction in Animal Kingdom is It's a Bugs Life, located in the Tree of Life. The part with the wasp sting and the beetles running under your butt freak and gross me out, so I'm not a huge fan.

> **TIP!** Book a character breakfast for the Fab Five or any characters that are must sees on your list. Before *Frozen* fever and the addition of Anna and Elsa, Mickey could garner some pretty hefty lines. Annie is our characters fan, but the rest of the kids were really not into hanging out in a long line for a photo and autograph. Doing a character breakfast meant Nate got his bacon, Austin his morning sugar fix, and Annie had time to give Mickey multiple hugs.

The beauty of having the grandparents along was date night. Now that the kids are older, date night is easy and the older kids can even take the younger ones into the park, but at the time it would have been a night in the room if it weren't for Grandma and Grandpa. All of us ended up at

Epcot, probably because it was such an easy walk. Joe and I considered many options, but decided to eat at Les Chefs de France again as our taste buds needed that creamy, sweet lobster bisque.

Have a date on your trip if you can. I get it. You feel guilty. It's a family vacation, right? Well, your spouse is part of the family, too, and it's important to take a little time for the two of you, even if it's just an hour to go for a walk. Disney World can be a very romantic place and seeing it with a pair of "grown-up, I'm here with my best friend" eyes is worth it.

CHAPTER FOUR
Mickey's Very Merry Christmas

Day 6

Day six was bright and sunny, though still cool, and filled with anticipation for Mickey's Very Merry Christmas party at the Magic Kingdom. We knew it would be a great party, but we never imagined how great. We took our time in the morning and arrived at the park in the early afternoon. Our first stop was Mickey and Minnie's pads in Toontown. Sadly, they're no longer at Disney World. These houses provided a lot of fun for Annie and Austin. They nosed through Minnie's fridge and invaded her tea party, while Joe rested in Minnie's chair. We also got to rummage through Mickey's house and check out his holiday decorations. Austin convinced us all to ride Goofy's Barnstormer, a child-friendly roller coaster with wacky sounds, twists, and turns. It's about as goofy as its namesake. If you have young ones in your group, Goofy's Barnstormer is a great first roller-coaster ride.

After battling Zurg at Buzz Lightyear's Space Ranger Spin, it was time for dinner at Cinderella's Royal Table. As we were walking into the castle a few soldiers for Mickey's Very Merry were heading out, which fueled the excitement for the party to come. But first, time to hang with some princesses.

Cinderella is actually located in the lobby area of the castle, before you enter the restaurant. Annie got her Cinderella autograph and picture and then we all headed upstairs to the dining area. The dining room feels quite royal, with a high ceiling and ornate columns. The stained-glass windows have reds, yellows, and royal blues, and you can see the rooftops of Fantasyland in the distance. It really does feel like you are in a castle, with a village of small homes just outside your dining room window. For dessert we had ice cream adorned with a tiny chocolate crown that gave a nice crunch to the creamy vanilla deliciousness. The most memorable moment was when Jasmine entered the room. Every dad in the room tried to be discreet when checking her out, while the boys at our table asked for an autograph just for the chance to talk to her.

Mickey had quite an act to follow after Jasmine, but he delivered with one heck of a Christmas party.

There are few places as magical as Disney World at Christmas. The parades, food, and decorations put you into the holiday mood. During the research and planning phase of this trip, I was surprised to learn all that was offered. Even before *Frozen*, the Magic Kingdom was an incredible place to be at the holidays. I remember having read about Mickey's Very Merry Christmas Party in a guidebook, but was struggling to even find information online, let alone buy tickets. Now there are an abundance of online resources and books devoted just to Disney World at Christmas. One of my favorites, by Ken Bingham and aptly titled *Walt Disney Christmas 2014*, transports you into the parks and hotels, and describes an array of different holiday activities. He even has some interesting personal stories and anecdotes thrown in.

We were lucky during this trip—not only because we could experience all the holiday fun that Disney has to offer, but also we were there at a time when the crowds were manageable. I was able to score tickets to Mickey's Very Merry Christmas Party and the Candlelight Processional, and enjoyed many of the festivities with short (or no) lines and perfect views.

> **TIP!** If you are visiting Disney World during the holiday season, the weeks leading up to Christmas are some of the busiest of the year. Definitely buy tickets to Mickey's Very Merry Christmas Party so you can enjoy a lot of the rides at Magic Kingdom that you may miss because of lines. If your budget allows it, you may even want to go to the party twice, the first time to see all the parades, shows, and fireworks, and the other to hit all the attractions. Keep in mind that not every attraction is open during the party, but most are. If you have the money, you could even do one of the many tours. There's one that takes you to key attractions in all four parks and another where you're taken behind the scenes to learn how Disney decorates for the holidays.

Everywhere you go at Disney World, from the parks to the resorts, there is holiday magic. The decorations at Beach Club and Yacht Club made a beautiful backdrop for our wedding photos. There was a huge Christmas tree at the Beach Club that almost reached the ceiling and was decorated with soft white twinkle lights, large golden sailboats, and bright teal-and-cream-colored ornaments of sea horses and fish. The life-size carousel made entirely of chocolate and gingerbread looked like a tasty treat and added a sweet, creamy, slightly spicy scent to the air. The Christmas tree in the sunroom at the Beach Club Villas featured soft white twinkle lights, ribbons of red and gold, small sparkling snowflakes, and even small bouquets of little white flowers.

At the Yacht Club there were Christmas trees drenched in nautical-themed ornaments and ribbons, garland strung along the banisters of the grand staircase, and a miniature train set that zoomed around a snow-covered mountain and village. Austin, still at the height of his *Thomas the Tank Engine* stage, really loved this.

Epcot has so many holiday festivities and decorations you could spend days savoring the treats, posting decorations on Pinterest, and exploring the way holidays are celebrated around the world. On our walk over to Epcot from the Beach Club Villas, there were bright green garlands with vivid red ribbons wrapped around the posts. We caught the performance of the tall, brightly dressed Pere Noel in France. He draws a crowd, and many laughs, with his animated storytelling. All around World Showcase there are holiday decorations in the style of each country. Some are quite understated—like the wreath in the sunroom at Les Chefs de France bistro with its twinkle lights and small pink and gold baubles. My favorite was the Christmas tree right near the entrance to World Showcase. It was gigantic, with oversized decorations including globes, brightly colored baubles, bells, and festive signs saying Merry Christmas in many different languages.

Another tree in Epcot featured oversized gifts wrapped to represent the different countries in World Showcase. One was red with the Canadian maple leaf. Another had bright purple wrapping with a magenta ribbon and a large tag with the Epcot logo. The tree was covered in bright white lights and candy treats—huge candy canes, bright blue balls that looked like gumballs, and white, fluffy, toasted marshmallows the size of small basketballs. We had plans to attend the Candlelight Processional and had booked the dinner package, with Restaurant Marrakesh. However, as we approached the pavilion, drizzle and a long line of damp people greeted us. And that was just to get into the theater. The decision was unanimous: skip standing in the rain and instead play in World Showcase and then watch the Holiday Illuminations show.

We took a lot of photos on this trip and were lucky enough to have two albums to bring back the memories. Digging through those albums I was able to relive all the different touches around Disney-MGM Studios, like the wreath on the wall at 50's Prime Time Cafe and the festive planters with bright red ribbons dotted around the park. One thing we enjoyed was all the holiday merchandise. We tried on Minnie ears with little Santa hats. Joe looked quite festive in his large Santa hat that featured a plush Christmas tree completely decorated with small Christmas-dressed Disney characters. All on one hat! Austin found a small stuffed dog wearing a cute holiday plaid hat and scarf.

The most memorable tree was at Animal Kingdom. It was so high that it couldn't even fit into photos and was decorated with hand-carved ornaments in muted tones of beige, gold, and gray. There were wooden stars as tall as Austin with lions, rhinos, and hidden Mickeys scattered throughout. Annie especially loved the characters from Winnie the Pooh that surrounded the base of the tree. The Christmas magic was all around and even the characters were in on the action. At our character breakfast at Restaurantosaurus, the Fab Five were in holiday garb. Goofy sported brightly colored ornaments dangling from his safari hat. Mickey—always the trendsetter—had donned an ugly Christmas sweater before they were even a "thing." In 2005, an ugly Christmas sweater was just something you would see your kid's teacher wearing.

Imagine, you've just finished your dinner, it's now dark, you're walking around trying to decide how to burn some time before Fantasmic!, and you walk right into the middle of over 5 million Christmas lights strung about two block of city streets in Disney-MGM Studios. Holiday music floods the air, snow is floating all around, and the lights cover every square inch of the buildings with figures along the rooftops. There were streets of lights to explore and every time you turned a corner, you were greeted by twinkling lights in every color of the rainbow. Think of that Christmas lights-obsessed neighbor or the houses on the HGTV Christmas Lights special. Now times that by 10, add some Disney magic, and you can start to image how incredible this was. Everyone started running around like crazy through the streets, taking pictures and exclaiming about the lights. Nate made the mistake of tasting the snow, learning quickly it is soap bubbles and not the crunchy cold white stuff back home in the frozen tundra of Chicago. One of the best photos is of Joe, the kids, and me all standing with the colorful world of Christmas behind us and huge grins of joy on our faces. When you look at this photo you don't see evil stepmothers or stepsisters, you see a family, enjoying Christmas magic, courtesy of Disney.

Each park and resort adds its own special touch to the holiday magic, but the ultimate is Magic Kingdom and Mickey's Very Merry Christmas Party. It all starts as you stroll down Main Street. There are garlands with fairy lights everywhere, strung across the buildings and twinkling along the windows of Crystal Palace. Even Mickey and Minnie's houses in Toontown had a strand of golf ball-size multi-color lights hung "haphazardly" along the outside. It looked as if Mickey had been up on a ladder decorating his house for the season. Even Cinderella had decorated the inside of her castle for guests on their way to Cinderella's Royal Table. She was wearing her signature blue gown, but for photos she knelt in front of a stunning Christmas tree covered in twinkle lights, gold ribbon, and bright blue ornaments for a small shock of color. Bright red poinsettia plants in large cream-colored planters surrounded the tree. It was understated elegance, just as you would expect in a castle at Christmas.

After lunch was our first of a few parades of the day. This one had many of the traditional floats, but they were decked out for the holidays with garlands, bows, and characters in holiday garb. The kids were all at the height of their *Toy Story* craze so the float resembling Andy's room—with a green garland, red-and-white striped bows, and brightly colored ornaments—was a huge hit. The baking elves from Santa's Workshop were dressed in bright green dresses with red-and-white striped hats and sleeves. I always feel for the folks in these parades. I get that the North Pole is chilly, but Florida mid-day is a steamy place and the fact that the performers can dance in long sleeves covered in make-up and still have smiles on their faces shows a true commitment to the performance. This parade even featured the "big man" himself in his sleigh, perched, very precariously I might add, on a chimney high above the crowd.

As the sun started to set, the park took on an air of anticipation as the party neared. Even the cast members seemed excited as we started to see more and more of them donning holiday accessories. I waited near Tomorrowland to get our Mickey's party wristbands, listening to everyone talking excitedly about what was to come. As darkness fell, the park transformed into a winter wonderland. Snowflakes fell around Cinderella Castle. Holiday singers in Victorian holiday costumes sang at the gazebo on Main Street, the men in top hats and the women in red bonnets with complementary white snowflakes. We made our way to Big Thunder Mountain as the ropes started to go up and guests not attending the party were encouraged to make their final purchases at the Emporium and depart.

Mickey's Very Merry Christmas Party had begun. It was as if there was a holiday scent piped in as the free cookies and hot chocolate started flowing. Our festivities started by grabbing our first of many cookies and hot chocolate at the station between Liberty Square and Fantasyland. We used the first hours of the party to dash from ride to ride in Fantasyland. Within an hour, we rode Peter Pan's Flight, Dumbo, Snow White's Scary Adventures, and the Many Adventures of Winnie the Pooh, and watched Mickey's PhilharMagic.

As parade time approached, we grabbed our spot along the end of the bridge near the castle at the edge of Liberty Square. Joe came skipping down the bridge quickly and ran right into the rope set up for the parade. His memory of this day is the bruises along the top of his thighs. It was nothing another cookie and some cocoa couldn't cure!

Mickey's Very Merry Christmas Parade was a mix of Disney magic and holiday classics—with a dash of Spectromagic thrown in. As the parade neared its end, the castle transformed once again to look as if it was dripping in icicles. This was before Elsa and her ice castle, but looking back at the photos one could see this may have been an inspiration.

As Holiday Wishes: Celebrate the Spirit of the Seasons, the holiday-themed fireworks show began, we stood in the crowd on Main Street near Crystal Palace entranced by the exploding sky and festive soundtrack. Nate stuck out his tongue, once again forgetting that Disney snow, though magical looking, was not so magical tasting. As we stood together, now officially a family, I let out a happy sigh, Joe rubbed his aching thigh, Nate took a bite of his Mickey ice cream, Mom whispered, "Can we go on Space Mountain?," Maggie took a selfie (with her plastic portable film camera), Annie hugged her stuffed Minnie, Bob snapped a photo, and Austin asked "Can I buy something now?"

Day 7

After a long night of holiday partying and parades, we were ready for something a bit more low key on our final day, so we headed to Downtown Disney for shopping, shopping, and more shopping. Our first stop was the Disney Days of Christmas store where we stocked up for the coming holiday. We bought a Victorian-style Mickey and Minnie ornament and a box set of ornaments that featured the symbols for each park. Then it was to World of Disney, the huge store that carried every Disney souvenir ever made. We picked up a photo album for our family and my parents, coloring books, t-shirts, and picture frames. I bought a few sets of the white chunky Mickey hands for some friends from work. When someone got out of line, we would whack each other with them.

"Can I buy this?" were the four words we heard constantly throughout the trip from Annie and Austin. We gave each kid a daily allowance, which was way too high (hey, we were excited) so they spent like crazy, and Nate even indulged a bit. So, in addition to our clothes, we had to find room for the souvenirs we couldn't resist:

- Mickey and Minnie stuffed animals we still have to this day

- A stuffed Woody

- A sword and Viking helmet

- Mickey ears with a little sorcerer's hat

- Annie's autograph book

- A Stitch hoodie for Austin, and a Beatles hoodie for Nate. Nate excitedly walked over to the UK pavilion at Epcot by himself and purchased it. He still has and wears that sweatshirt.

- Disney occasionally publishes souvenir books about the parks. At the time these were tricky to find outside of the parks, so we purchased and gave as a gift for the family at Christmas both the *Happiest Celebration on Earth* souvenir book and the *Walt Disney World: Where Dreams Come True* five-book box set. This set includes a book on each park and one on the water parks and the hotels.

Our last stop was the store at the Beach Club to pick up our packages from the in-park shopping. While there, Nate spotted the movie *Sky High* and asked, "Can we just stay in and watch a movie?" So instead of heading over to BoardWalk we spent our Saturday night, our last night at Disney, crammed into the living room of our villa watching *Sky High*. To this day, every one of the kids remembers that night. Looking around the room and seeing Maggie munching on cereal at the table, Annie and Nate crammed on the couch, and Austin playing with toys because he couldn't sit still through a whole movie, this (not-so) evil stepmother saw a family.

CHAPTER FIVE
Not-So-Evil Stepmother Disney Secret #1

Pre-booking Decisions

So you have one person who loves water parks, and the other ten don't…

On our 2015 trip it wasn't the evil stepmother, it was the evil mother. The hardest part of a Disney vacation is what you *aren't* going to do. Some families regularly visit the parks, so they just say "next time." In our case, we visit maybe every 5 years and only once every 10 years with the whole crew. In our case, Austin (a 15-year-old boy during our 2015 trip) loves the water parks. Not a single other person in our group had any interest in them at all. Do we cave and have everyone go? Split up? Austin wasn't quite at the age that we wanted him going to a park completely on his own, and dragging ten people somewhere they don't want to go wasn't the recipe for a fun trip.

Solution? We had a free half-day where everyone chose what they wanted to do. Austin actually decided he wanted to ride Rock 'n' Roller Coaster and do some shopping. Of course, him being him, he decided as we were relaxing by the pool at our hotel, after Hollywood Studios and visiting the Boardwalk Inn, that he wanted to go to Blizzard Beach. That's when I lost the Disney Mom award because I said no. It was the first time we had sat down since arriving four days earlier and we were going to Magic Kingdom for Wishes that night. I learned that three destinations in one day was daunting, exhausting, and only for the young'uns.

Where you stay during your Disney trip is important. You may think it's just the place you sleep and you wont be there much anyway, but at Disney it's more than the bed, it's the transportation, the savings, and the perks that make it worth staying on site. If your budget permits, stay at a Disney resort. But, which Disney resort? There are more than 25 Disney-operated resorts in Disney World, so looking at the list can be a bit overwhelming. Simplify the decision by asking yourself these five questions:

Question 1. What's my budget? Your budget will determine which category of Disney hotel you can afford:

- Value (the most affordable), which includes Pop Century, Art of Animation, and the All Stars
- Moderate, which includes Port Orleans, Caribbean Beach, and Coronado Springs
- Deluxe (the most expensive), which includes the Polynesian, the Grand Floridian, and the Contemporary, plus the many Disney Vacation Club (DVC) properties

In addition, there's the Swan and the Dolphin, which I have heard at Christmas time is a great place to be. I've stayed at the Dolphin for a springtime convention and wasn't a huge fan.

Question 2. What size room do you need? If you have a bigger party and a DVC villa is an option, I'd recommend it. The extra space, extra bathrooms, and the room to store snacks have always come in handy for us. In 2015 we stayed at Kidani Village. The room had three bathrooms three bathrooms and when you are traveling with nine, four of them women, that third bathroom is a necessity. The Beach Club 2-bedroom villa only had two bathrooms. Also, depending on the size of your party, some villas and hotel rooms are not large enough. This is where calling Disney and talking through options before making your list is helpful. I had even explored the possibility of renting a few hotel rooms, but learned Disney can't guarantee adjoining rooms, so that was out.

Question 3. In which parks will you spend most of your time? If you are staying for seven days and have plenty of time to see everything, spending hours on Disney buses may not be a huge issue. But, if you have 4 days, being able to walk to a park or having multiple ways of getting to a park may be a worthwhile investment. We always visit Magic Kingdom more than once, so staying at one of the hotels near that park has its benefits.

Question 4. What meals will you be eating at the hotel? Disney carries the theming into every part of the hotel—from the rooms to the pools to the dining. You can savor amazing flavors while giraffes saunter by at Sanaa at Animal Kingdom Lodge (AKL), have BBQ while your child competes in a horse race at Wilderness Lodge, and eat fresh sushi at the Polynesian. Even the room service at most of the hotels can offer new taste experiences, like the delicious and creamy Tandoori nachos at AKL's Kidani Village.

If you plan on eating most of your meals in your room to save money, make sure the room has kitchen facilities. Something we learned the hard way is that not all resorts have an abundance of food options. Some of the villa resorts, for example, may not have a quick service or breakfast option other than room service, which is pricey. One of the huge benefits of Bay Lake Tower was its easy access to the Contemporary Resort and all the food options there. However, getting from Kidani Village (limited food options, including nowhere to eat breakfast) to Jambo House at AKL (with many delicious options) was over a 1.5-mile walk or a bus ride to the hotel. On the other hand, watching my picky 15-year-old develop a love for butter chicken and naan while a zebra looked on was one of our most memorable moments of our 2015 trip, courtesy of Sanaa at Kidani Village. The Beach Club offers a ton of options between the those on the BoardWalk and in nearby Epcot—within 5 minutes you can be enjoying *pain au chocolat* in the France pavilion. I've heard a lot of folks say they love the Polynesian for many reasons, one being the many tasty and affordable food options.

Question 5. Do you want to be able to escape the crowds once you are at your hotel? This is something often forgotten when booking a room at Disney. There are many hotels with incredible pools, amazing restaurants, great shops, and monorail access. But these hotels also become destinations for many people who aren't actually hotel guests. We view our hotel as a sanctuary, an escape from the crowds. Sometimes you want to walk back from the pool in your swimsuit and towel, but if you have to walk through a lobby with a few hundred tourists, you may reconsider. I've always wanted to stay at the Polynesian, but after having dinner at the restaurant in their lobby and seeing the crowds and the noise, it would just be too much at the end of a long day at the parks. That's one of the benefits of many of the villa hotels like Kidani Village, Beach Club, and Bay Lake: they have their own entrances and fewer "touristy" features, and so attract fewer crowds. This is also what my parents loved about Coronado Springs.

There are a lot of decisions to make before a Disney vacation. We've talked about where to sleep, so now it's time to talk about "what are you going to do" and "where you are going to eat."

When booking your Disney hotel, you will also want to buy your park tickets. To do this, you need to have a pretty good idea of the number of days you are going to spend in the parks and what parks you will visit. This will help you determine whether you need a park hopper (the park hopper is a type of ticket that lets you go between different parks on the same day). If you are traveling with a big group that has been to Disney World before, ask everyone for the top three things they want to do, making no promises other than you will do your best to accommodate them. You will know which rides need a FP+ (FastPass), which requests you may not be able to fulfill, and which restaurants are on the list—important information because dining is one of the first things you book after booking your hotel/tickets package.

The crowd calendar on easywdw.com will help you determine which days are best to visit which parks. This is also when you will get a better sense of needing that park hopper. During our 2015 trip our free day was Wednesday, where one group went to Epcot, one to Hollywood Studios, and then we all went later to the Magic Kingdom. In that one day the Park Hopper proved its worth.

Now you want to have a rough idea of which park you'll visit on each day. For our group, I always schedule us for at least two days at Magic Kingdom. It is the park that has the most attractions we want to see, and so splitting our time over two days is less exhausting.

At this stage, I add in the meals so I know which Disney reservations to make. We always do Sci-Fi Dine-In at Hollywood Studios and in 2015 really wanted to eat at Be Our Guest. Since a Be Our Guest reservation is so hard to get, I knew we would need to be flexible and go when we could get seats.

I'd recommend only one big experience meal a day, so if you do a character breakfast, maybe save Be Our Guest or Sci-Fi Dine-In Theater for another time. It's also worth it to have a rough idea of where you want to eat your main meals each day. Breakfast for us is typically in the room, with one character breakfast per trip. Lunch is usually the big meal of the day; we use it to take a breather and relax. We've done Cinderella's Royal Table, Crystal Palace, Be Our Guest, or Sci-Fi Dine-In for lunch. Dinner can be a good time to try out resort restaurants. Sanaa and Jiko are huge favorites because they offer exotic tastes. With all the different resort theming, it is an incredible opportunity to try something new and make your Disney experience even more magical by hearing the pickiest eater in your group state something like, "I love naan."

Make sure you have at least one meal a day where your whole group is together and is focused on being together, not distracted by Tigger or *Attack of the 50-Foot Woman*. Meals really are a time to connect, talk about what you've seen, and remind yourself why you are at Disney World in the first place: to be together.

CHAPTER SIX
Not-So-Evil Stepmother
Disney Secret #2

Paying, and Saving, the Big Bucks

So you have a budget based on staying at a certain Disney resort, and it's booked…

We always stay at a Disney resort. If your budget allows, it's worth it. A lot of folks just look at the cost of the Disney hotel and say "can't afford it," but then end up renting a car, paying for parking, eating all their meals in the parks, and having an exhausting vacation because it's too far and too much money to take a break.

Solution? Once you have decided to stay at Disney, create a list of at least three hotels, ranked in order of preference before you call to make your reservations.

When I was planning our 2005 trip, we weren't really sure where to stay and the friendly Disney cast member on the phone gave us the great recommendation of the Beach Club Villas. When Joe and I took our son Oliver in 2013, I had done the research and knew we wanted to be able to walk to Magic Kingdom. Bay Lake Tower was within budget and walking distance of that park. The 2015 trip booking did not go as well. Thus far I had been spoiled, always able to book the hotel I wanted. It came as a bit of a shock when Beach Club Villas was a no go. The options we were given by the Disney reservations cast member were, first, Old Key West, which was within budget, had a good amount of floor space for our big party, but wasn't anywhere near the parks and not really themed in a way that appealed to us, and second, a bungalow at the Polynesian—let's just say that $40,000 was *way* above our budget. Though the bungalows look super cool, until that price comes down, a lot, it's not happening.

Our third and final option was Kidani Village at Animal Kingdom Lodge and at first it was an emphatic no. It wasn't within walking distance, or some-other-type-of-travel-method besides bus, from a park. We had been so spoiled from our last few trips with everything working out. This is when I learned a valuable lesson of having your priority list of locations before you call, otherwise you may end up making a rash decision for fear of not getting a room at all or have the bad luck of speaking to a cast member going through a bad day and lacking the patience to offer suggestions. All is well that ends well, though, and Kidani Village ended up being the right resort for us. With nine people, it had the space that we needed.

It was during our 2005 trip that we decided to invest in a car service to take us to and from the airport. Previously, we had used Disney's Magical Express transportation service, and it was great. The bus showed Disney movies, was themed, and we only had to wait at the airport for a few minutes. The ride in was nice, but our room wasn't ready and so when we finally saw our luggage again, we discovered my wedding dress bag had just been thrown onto a luggage cart and was completely wrinkled. Not a high point and not the wonderful folks at Magic Express' fault, but if we had been with our luggage, I could have informed the bell staff that the cream white bag saying wedding dress on it should be handled with care.

But the nail in the Magical Express coffin for us happened on our way back to the airport. After waiting for 40 minutes *after* the time we were *supposed* to be picked up, we asked the folks at Beach Club for help. They weren't able to give us (or the 30 or so other people looking concerned about missing their flight) any information on the arrival of our bus. After waiting 50 minutes, we called a taxi and a few minutes before it arrived a Magical Express bus finally pulled in—a bus already packed to the brim. We took a look at the long line of guests trying to figure out how they were going to squeeze themselves and their baggage on the over-crowded bus, got in our taxi, and vowed to never use Magical Express again.

On our 2013 and 2015 trips, we used a company called Happy Limousine and were pleased. They will even do a stop at a grocery store, Walgreens, or CVS on the way in so you can stock up on toiletries and snacks and bottled drinks. Eating breakfast in the room for a few days, not calling room service for a late night snack, not buying sunscreen at the pool, and avoiding a few snacks and drinks in the park will far make up for the $250 or so this will cost you. With our group of 11 in 2015, it also meant we were all together in one vehicle when seeing the Walt Disney World sign for the first time. Not only did we have a big church van we all fit in, they had a trailer for our luggage. I have heard from many folks that they love Magical Express and have had not one issue. With the security lines at Orlando airport always being pretty long and traveling with multiple children, running through an airport is not high on my list. So the expense of the van was well worth it.

We have learned a great way to save money at Disney: the Disney Visa from Chase. Using that card saved us *over $1300* on our last vacation.

The trick was Joe and I both got one card each. He did the premium and I did not. Here's how these cards saved us more money than we both had thought: Joe got $200 back on his first purchase over $500 and no interest for 6 months on our Disney vacation; I got $50 back on my first purchase. Each card returned a % back that we could put on Disney rewards cards, which are like gift cards you can use pretty much anywhere in the parks. Joe got 2% back on all purchases before our trip, so between the pre-vacation purchases and paying for our vacation using the card, we had a Disney rewards card with about $400 on it. My 1% back totaled a $250 rewards card and we took both cards to the parks with us.

Now these are both conservative estimates, but with 10% off merchandise in the park we estimate it saved us at least $100. With 10% off certain meals, our one meal at Jiko alone saved us $85. The 10% discount on meals saved us well over $250. Joe also got 2% back on all those purchases made in the park, so that was mother $50 on the rewards card and for me another $40 in rewards that we used on disneystore.com back home for Christmas presents. A $1300 savings on a Disney vacation is a secret I'm shouting from the rooftops.

Experience 2007: Disney for 2

Yes! One bite, and all your dreams will come true.
—Evil Queen, *Snow White and the Seven Dwarfs*

CHAPTER SEVEN
Swans, Spoodles, and Showcase

Sometimes, if you're really lucky, you get to visit Disney for work. In 2007, I had to be at Disney for a work conference, and Joe headed south to hang with me. It was my sixth trip to Disney and Joe's fourth. Since we had just been there in 2005, Joe and I had one Disney experience on our mind: food.

The conference location and my home for the week was the Dolphin. Although convenient for a conference or a trade show, it is not on the top of my list of Disney resorts, for a number of reasons, including the lack of Disney theming, the sheer size of the building, and the sub-par service and view. On the other hand, the location can't be beat: it's a short boat ride to Epcot and Hollywood Studios; plus, you're just steps away from the BoardWalk.

This was a trip that was all about the food. The first night we made the trek across the walkway over to the Swan and tried out Kimono. The karaoke performances have a stronger hold on my memory than the food. It was the standard set of YMCA, Sinatra, and of course, the bachelorette party with tiaras and drunken pack behavior giggling their way through "Girls Just Want to Have Fun."

The next night we had dinner at a restaurant that I'm sad to say is no longer there. Spoodles was a small-plates venue with outdoor seating at the Boardwalk Inn. For a state with such warm weather (I'm from Chicago where it can go from 35°F to 65°F in a day), there is a lack of restaurants offering outdoor dining at Disney World. Seeing as it was about 45°F back home and almost 80°F in Orlando, outdoor dining was high on our list of criteria that night. Spoodles was replaced by celebrity chef Cat Cora's Kouzzina, which also closed. The space is now occupied by Trattoria al Forno.

But back to 2007 and a dinner we actually remember. We had a romantic table outside overlooking Crescent Lake (which connects the Epcot hotels and Hollywood Studios). Spoodles featured small plates, my favorite way to eat. I love a meal where you can have a few bites of a lot of different tastes. Small plates have become quite the trend, inspired by the Spanish tapas-style cuisine of Barcelona. I specifically remember this was the first time I had mussels with chorizo, a delicious combination. The spiciness in the chorizo actually brings out the sweetness in the mussels. The dish also included sweet cherry tomatoes and fresh crusty bread that you could dip in the flavorful broth.

TIP! Disney is not just for kids. You can have just as much fun without the kids. We always enjoyed our "alone" time there. For some couples, it's the opportunity to see shows your kids won't sit through, hit thrill rides they're too young for, have a nice dinner at a World Showcase restaurant they won't eat in, or just have a date walking around and seeing details you may have missed when you're pushing a stroller or wrangling your group.

On our last night we went back to one of our favorites from our 2005 trip, Les Chefs de France in Epcot. Joe and I strongly considered treating ourselves and trying Bistro de Paris (now called Monsieur Paul), an upscale French restaurant located on the floor above Les Chefs. Then we both remembered the lobster bisque from two years prior and decided that we couldn't resist it. The bisque comes with a gigantic soup spoon and a crusty baguette. The baguette keeps you classy as you can use that instead of your fingers or your face to get the last sweet lobster goodness before your waiter comes and whisks your plates away. This meal involved a glass (or two) of some bubbly and a tasty dessert before our walk back to the Beach Club to catch the boat and our last long trek to our room at the Dolphin.

CHAPTER EIGHT
Not-So-Evil Stepmother Disney Secret #3

Building Excitement for Your Disney Trip

Getting your "Disney" on before you leave home can be a fun way to extend the vacation. There are so many ways to get excited and start engaging with Disney in advance of your trip. With so much out there, how do you decide what to spend your time on?

If you've done Disney before and read the guidebooks, find some blogs that tell you what's new. I don't really read guidebooks any more. I did for our first big trip for our wedding in 2005. Often, though, the Disney guidebooks start to sound the same: ride statistics, explaining the hub, defining "guest" and "cast member," etc.

If it's *your* first Disney trip, read a book geared to Disney World first-timers, like Dave Shute and Josh Humphrey's *The Easy Guide to Your Walt Disney World Visit* (a 2017 edition is available). Both authors also maintain useful, active sites: Dave's is yourfirstvisit.net, Josh's is easywdw.com.

Also, call Disney. It may take more than one call, but you will eventually get that Disney reservation agent who is a super fan and who will have a ton of tips and tell you exactly where to go. I have gotten some of the best dining and hotel tips from just having a friendly conversation with a reservation agent. Many of them are Disney fanatics.

With the wide age range of our group, we used a lot of different ways to build the anticipation for the magic. There are whole websites of ideas for building Disney excitement, just Google "you're going to Disney World" and you can entertain yourself for hours on YouTube alone. Here are a few ideas that worked for us:

- Ordering MagicBands. All nine of us crowded around the laptop and debated the colors a few months prior to the trip. When the bands came, I took a picture and sent it to all the kids who were no longer living at home.

- Joe, Oliver and I created a calendar counting down the days to the trip. We did ours two weeks out. As the trip neared, we wrote the specific things we were looking forward to, like "4 days to Expedition Everest!" The calendar became a huge hit for everyone in the family.

- My dad is a photographer, so for Father's Day I searched high and low for a photographer's guide to Disney World. Now some of you may be reading this saying, "there's this book by so and so." I consider myself fairly internet and Amazon savvy and found nothing. I ended up creating my own through a combination of some cool blogs, websites, and Shutterfly. There are some incredible sites out there, and many of the photographers will reveal technical details like aperture and the camera they were using.

- Oliver got a journal called the *Kid's Travel Journal: Disney Edition*. It had a fun pre-trip section that asked, "What do I want to see and do on my trip?" Oliver answered: "Expedition Everest, Mission: SPACE, giraffes, Mickey, and skipping."

- All holidays leading up to our Disney trips involved some sort of Disney-related gift (and most holiday since have as well). For my birthday, Joe and the kids got me a cute robin's egg blue Hershel backpack for me to use in the parks. He wisely purchased a bag in a neutral color that even the boys didn't mind carrying. The bag was decorated with Mickey and Minnie pins and contained a portable phone charger. That charger came in very handy. It can charge 2–3 mobile phones at a time, and if you remember to plug it in every night, it can make it through a long day in the parks.

- Nate, Sam, and I spent a lot of time looking at the menus from Epcot's Food & Wine Festival preparing our taste buds for the deliciousness to come. Sam and I sent quite a few texts about the magical munchies we were going to try. Annie did some online digging to identify every place in all four parks where she could find Tigger. Oliver showed great patience when the planning DVD came, waiting until his brothers and sisters were ready to watch it. My mom even called me after they watched theirs. But the best thing we did was looking at photo albums, sharing our happiest Disney memories, and anticipating all the new magic we would create.

And sometimes it's nothing you do, it's just life that gets your kids excited. In late September, after a long day at school and then cheer practice, Austin said to me, "You know how they say it's the place where dreams come true and you can be a kid again? I love Disney because I feel like I can be a kid again. I just have such good memories there. You can escape and be away from everything. You get to go and just play. I'm really excited for Disney." We then spent the rest of the car ride talking about memories from previous trips and what we are looking forward to.

That's what Disney does for families. It sparks conversation; it's a way to connect that is positive. Disney is so magical it can even get a teenage boy talking (and if you have a teenage boy, you know how magical that is!).

Experience 2013: Disney for 3

No no no, it can't be.
I distinctly remember, your birthday was last year.

—Mother Gothel, *Tangled*

CHAPTER NINE
Bay Lake, Boats, and Birthdays

Can I go to Disney World?" asked a four-year-old Oliver one day after looking at pictures of our family (pre-Oliver) in front of the castle at Christmastime. Sounds like a plan.

Cast

- Oliver, celebrating his 5th birthday on his first trip to Disney World.
- Joe, also known as Dada, on his 5th trip to Disney World.
- Me, also known as Mama, on my 7th trip to Disney World.

Itinerary

- *Day 1.* We arrived on an early flight on Wednesday, May 8. After a little rest, we walked (yes, walked!) to the Magic Kingdom, then returned to the Contemporary for dinner at the Wave.
- *Day 2.* Hollywood Studios, with lunch at the Sci-Fi Dine-In Theater, dinner at the Tune-In Lounge, and snacks at Fantasmic!
- *Day 3.* Epcot, with Coco-Puffs in the stroller, lunch at Epcot's Flower & Garden food marketplaces, and dinner at Tutto Gusto Wine Cellar.
- *Day 4.* Animal Kingdom, with a character breakfast at Tusker House, a dim sum lunch at Yak & Yeti, and dinner with Lazy Susan at Whispering Canyon Café at Wilderness Lodge.
- *Day 5.* Oliver's birthday at Magic Kingdom, with breakfast at Gaston's, snacks by the hotel pool, and popcorn from a stand in Belle's village in Fantasyland.
- *Day 6.* Heading home.

When planning this trip, I knew Magic Kingdom would be a park we would visit more than once. So, I decided to try for a Magic Kingdom hotel. We had good experiences at Disney Vacation Club (DVC) villa hotels and decided to stay at one of them again. I read about Bay Lake Tower at Disney's Contemporary Resort and how you can see the Magic Kingdom fireworks from the bridge and how, most importantly, you can walk to the Magic Kingdom. We loved that we were able to walk to Epcot in 2005 and knew that being able to walk to and from Magic Kingdom would make napping possible, both for the grown-ups and for Oliver.

CHAPTER TEN
A Day of Magical Firsts

Day 1

Oliver had an overwhelming number of firsts on this day, so many that his cheeks hurt from smiling and excitement. This was his first plane ride, followed by his first monorail ride at the Orlando airport. It was our first time using a car service from the airport, and we are huge fans. They provided a car seat and made a pit stop at a Walgreens that had a mini grocery store inside, so we stocked up on snacks, breakfast treats, and drinks for the room.

As we approached the gates, Oliver was straining his skinny little neck to catch a peek. Seeing Mickey and the outline of the gates for Magic Kingdom was almost too much; he was almost bursting, despite being up at 3 a.m. to catch our flight. The car pulled up to Bay Lake Tower and we were greeted by a number of friendly cast members. The bubbly cast member checking us in made our day when he said our room was ready. He gave Oliver his birthday button and even dotted the eye with a hidden Mickey. Then he gave us a small packet with a whole new way of capturing character autographs: a poster that featured the castle surrounded by different Disney characters. Autograph books are fun, but you get them, maybe show a few friends, and then it gets tucked into a bookshelf. But this poster ended up covered with autographs and still hangs on Oliver's wall.

After dropping off our stuff, grabbing a snack, and freshening up, Oliver made it clear he was ready to hit the parks. We packed up our super-handy umbrella stroller, our new poster for autographs, and walked over to the Magic Kingdom.

Prior to this trip, I did my research and purchased a Walt Disney World guidebook written for kids. This book was fantastic and served as an excitement builder prior to the trip, as well as a guidebook and journal during the trip. It has pictures of the sun for the weather and cartoon faces that kids can circle to show how they felt about an attraction. The back section has a bunch of fill-in-the-blank journal pages, with spaces for the attractions, souvenirs, food, hidden Mickeys, and favorite moments.

Oliver was way too excited to write, so I mostly filled it out with his input. The only drawback is the heftiness of the book; you need a backpack or stroller if you want to bring it into the parks.

Oliver had a selection of things he wanted to see, and Pirates of the Caribbean was high on his list. After grabbing a Lightning McQueen cookie the size of his head on Main Street and getting the standard pic in front of the castle, we went to Adventureland and our first of a few times on Pirates. "The guy with the bone is trying to get the dog to give him a key but the dog is like, no way," Oliver said, quickly followed by, "Can we do it again?" We heard this question a lot and just decided to go with it. There were quite a few attractions we rode more than once on this trip.

> **TIP!** Go with the flow when you can. Some of the best moments at Disney World are not planned. Make sure you have some time scheduled each day to just ask someone in your group what they want to do. Now, I prefer when our whole family is together, but one of the best parts of this trip was letting Oliver plan our days. That meant we rode Star Tours four times in a row and took over two hours for lunch at Sci-Fi Dine-In because he thought the trailer for *Attack of the 50-Foot Woman* that played on the "drive-in" screen was hysterical. It was a relief to have minimal parts of our day scheduled and to experience the magic Oliver style.

"I liked that I was at the top of the tree house," was the reason for Oliver's thumbs up for Swiss Family Treehouse. There are a few attractions that are definitely about tradition and this is one of them. None of our kids have even seen the movie, but there is something about a gigantic treehouse with rooms and elevators that makes you want to climb some trees. The trek through Adventureland continued over to Frontierland and our first of two trips on Big Thunder Mountain Railroad. This was Oliver's first roller coaster and he loved screaming at the top of his lungs as we hurtled over the hills and through the caves. We rode it again on Sunday at night and it was cooler because "there was hot lava at nighttime."

Haunted Mansion was just a bit too scary and received a thumb down because "I was scared of the stairs. I did like it when the ghost pulled Mama and Dada's heads off." This was the first time we experienced the new interactive queue. To keep guests occupied and happy while waiting in line, Disney has worked their magic on a number of attractions so that standing in line is actually fun. The Haunted Mansion queue is a bit like they stopped the ride and let you play in some of the rooms. At one "station" along the queue, called the Decomposing Composer's Crypt, there are a series of busts of characters from the ride that are a blast to pose with. Oliver and Joe had fun playing on the spooky instruments, like a pipe organ with skulls. My favorite was the large haunted bookshelf where the books moved and popped out. It's fun trying to push them back in.

Now that we had our hitchhiking ghost from Haunted Mansion, we back-tracked through the castle to Tomorrowland. Oliver thought this was so cool "because we got to walk through it." Our next stop was to sate Oliver's Buzz Lightyear craving. After blasting lasers and "trying our best," according to Oliver, we hit the Stitch ride (which was a meh for us all) then headed back toward Fantasyland and lighter fun.

Oliver was so excited and hadn't eaten enough so, smart parents that we are, we bought him a big ice cream. And then he threw up. Another Disney first for us all. That was our sign it was time to head back to the room. As we walked down Main Street, we caught the beginning of the afternoon parade and grabbed a prime location in the grassy area just outside town hall. Wearing the birthday button has many advantages and one of them was the number of characters in the parade that gave Oliver special attention. He got a high-five from Captain Hook. This was the height of his *Jake and the Neverland Pirates* kick and the Hook high-five was cause for screams of joy and a huge smile. There were also a number of blown kisses from princesses, happy birthday wishes from cast members, and a special wave from Mickey.

For dinner, we made the fast walk over to the Wave restaurant at the Contemporary. After having only a small snack from Friar's Nook in Fantasyland, our stomachs were letting us know it was time for dinner. We munched on some meats and cheeses, and Joe and I both enjoyed a grown-up cocktail while Oliver got his first of a few light-up cups. This is a pricey souvenir cup with a clip-on character that lights up. They are at most restaurants and feature popular characters.

Oliver had been saving up his allowance for months and we also gave him $15 a day as his birthday present, so shopping was high on the list. On our way back to the room, we stopped in one of the gift shops in the Contemporary lobby and added a few more goodies to the first-day purchases of a set of plastic Star Wars figures that came in an incredibly useful zip plastic case. They were a cuter version of the main characters. Both Darth Vader and Yoda actually made it back into the parks a few times. Oliver also got a blue vintage Mickey shirt and a keychain that looked like Buzz Lightyear's gun. This was also where we discovered the character packs. Similar to LEGO mini-figures, these packs have multiple series and then many characters within each series. Each one is a surprise and typically had 2–3 characters inside. There are ride vehicles from famous Disney attractions, princesses, *Star Wars*, and even holiday-themed packs. I enjoyed collecting them as much as Oliver did. We still have them and they're great for long car rides.

As we dragged ourselves back to our room we stopped on the bridge between the Contemporary and Bay Lake Tower. It offers a nice view of Cinderella Castle and Celebrate the Magic, a nighttime show at Magic Kingdom. During Celebrate the Magic, the castle becomes a canvas for Disney storytelling. A series of clips from Disney and Pixar films are projected right onto the castle. Prior to that moment, we didn't even know that this show existed. Despite the almost 18 hour day, the three of us stood entranced as Wreck-It-Ralph wrecked the castle, Mickey painted every brick in a rainbow of colors, the lanterns from *Tangled* floated into the sky, the balloons from *Up* reached the top of the highest tower, and the part that makes me tear up (even when I watch it on YouTube), the quote from Walt: "Never forget, it was all started by a mouse." Then we headed back to our room to pass out from exhaustion.

CHAPTER ELEVEN
Jedis, Mickey Hugs, and Babysitters

Day 2

Day two featured the most magical moment of our whole trip—all because of an amazing Jedi master.

The day started with Lucky Charms and a bus ride over to Hollywood Studios. Oliver is obsessed with *Star Wars*. While Joe and Oliver raced over to sign Oliver up for Jedi Academy, I grabbed Toy Story Mania FastPasses.

Our initial ride of the day was Star Tours, the first of four times. The coolest part of Star Tours is that each trip is different. From the guest in your cruiser who is identified as the Rebel spy, to visiting various locations from the films and having different adventures each time, no two tours are ever the same. During the motion-simulator ride, you visit a few of the destinations from the films. On our trips we visited the Wookie planet first, then Tatooine, and then the ultimate, the ice planet Hoth. Oliver's favorite movie is *The Empire Strikes Back* and Hoth was a huge hit. He told us, "Favorite ride ever."

Joe parted with well over $100 at Tatooine Traders where we picked out gifts for Annie and Nate and got Austin a fun shirt of Darth Vader on Prince Charming's Regal Carrousel with the quote: "This will be a day long remembered." Oliver made his own droid, which is a fun activity and a way to get out of the heat for a few minutes. The process can be long for some kids because there are so many options. I strongly suggest the more patient parent for this one.

> **TIP!** Use the Disney resort delivery services or you will have a sore back by the end of the day. Oliver could pick one new toy he could keep with him, but we sent the rest back to our resort. At most resorts, you pick up your items at the resort gift shop. We have used this service every trip and have never had an issue. It's also fun because it's like getting your goodies all over again when you pick them up later. And here's another tip: little boxes of cereal make great on-the-go

breakfasts. The multi-packs give variety over the course of a trip; if your child doesn't finish the box, you close it up, throw it in the bag, and you have quick snack and a good distraction while waiting in line.

Our next stop was to immerse ourselves in the world of Toy Story at Pixar Place. After pictures with some Army Men that happened to be scooting by, we rode Toy Story Mania, which Oliver "loved because I didn't have to shoot. We shot at aliens in the Buzz one and then Woody yelled be careful of the hat!" The line for Toy Story Mania is almost as cool as the ride itself. The feeling of being a small toy in an over-sized version of Andy's bedroom with all the games, toys, and details from the movie is so cool. The line for Toy Story Mania is one of the longest in all of Hollywood Studios. FastPasses are a must, but it's definitely a line worth stopping to soak up all the details.

One of my favorite character pics is of Oliver, Buzz, and Woody playing with Oliver's plastic Storm Trooper and Boba Fett. It was obvious that Buzz and Woody knew their *Star Wars*. The waiting area to meet them is indoors. It's a nice break from the beating sun and very interactive, with spaces resembling various scenes from the movie. Buzz and Woody hang out in a picturesque area that looks like Andy's bed, and both of them have a great time interacting and playing with the guests. After autographs, hugs, high fives, and a quick stop to purchase a talking Buzz Lightyear, it was off to lunch at Sci-Fi Dine-In Theater.

Sci-Fi is a must in our family. Of all the sit-down restaurants, this one is high up there in immersive experience. Sci-Fi is a burger-and-shakes place and they do that really well. The burgers are gigantic, the fries crispy, and the shakes thick and creamy. They even have cocktails for the grown-ups. Oliver got a hot dog and a Lightning McQueen punch that came with a clip on glowing Lightning. It can be chilly in Sci-Fi, so make sure you have a long-sleeved layer. It's dark in there, too, and you might be able to catch a quick cat nap while you wait for your food, especially if you have already seen *Attack of the 50-Foot Woman*. During lunch we talked about the rest of our day and seeing the Little Mermaid show, which Oliver was so excited about until I said it had puppets. "Puppets? It's puppets?" he said, almost disgusted. Now it was no "ice planet Hoth," but he really enjoyed the show and said that Ariel was pretty.

Disney Jr. Live on Stage offered another chance to sit down and cool off. The best part of the show was at the very end where all the characters are singing and dancing and they release gold "doubloons," the treasure from *Jake and the Neverland Pirates*. These doubloons are just circles of paper that are released from holders in the ceiling. As you look around the room and the colorful lights are dancing around, with the doubloons fluttering through the air and little kids looking up, it feels very Disney.

Then it was finally time: Jedi Academy. Oliver had been waiting all day. This experience starts with a group of about 15 kids meeting in a building near Star Tours. Here the kids meet with their guides and get their Padawan robes and instructions about what is going to happen. While the kids are receiving their instructions, the parents are in a separate area close to Star Tours, crowding around the stage where the training will take place. A PhotoPass photographer captures the entire thing and will give you a card with all the photos from the lesson. The photographer zooms back and forth on a track on the ground in front of the 4-foot-high stage.

As everyone jostles for position, the trainees start their walk to the stage. There is a whole line of them in brown robes with hoods. An assistant, who is usually a bit frazzled because the age range of the trainees can be pretty vast (from 4 to 12), brings them up on the stage. Then the Jedi Master comes out. He is typically a charismatic fellow with a great sense of humor who keeps the adults laughing and the kids engaged. Oliver was about a head shorter than the next smallest kid, so he got a prime training location in front. The Jedi Master passes out the lightsabers and teaches the kids how to activate them and do a number of specific moves. Oliver struggled a bit, but he looked adorable with his huge cheeks and big blue eyes, and the Jedi Master gave him some extra help.

Then, just as they are almost ready, familiar music starts playing and through a cloud of smoke, Darth Vader and two Stormtroopers appear through a door at the back of the stage. The Jedi Master rushes the kids to safety on the side of the stage while Darth Vader tries to convince them to come to the dark side, requiring each of them to battle him. Just about the time Darth Vader appears, the kid standing next to Oliver lets out this wail in sheer terror. Up to that point, Oliver was doing great and ready for battle. After hearing a kid a few years older and bigger than him break down, we knew he was thinking, "Well, that kid's scared and he's bigger than me, so maybe I should be scared, too." We could see the fear on his face.

The assistant saw Oliver starting to cry and kept moving him to the end of the line. Joe and I stood in the audience as our little man looked at us, scared out of his gourd, knowing how disappointed he would be if he didn't get to try. Just as it seemed all hope was lost for him to have a chance to battle Darth Vader, the Jedi Master came over, knelt down in front of him, and said the magic words (which we still don't know because Oliver told us it was for Jedis only). After a few seconds, he walked out on stage with Oliver to the roar of the crowd. Everyone had been watching with bated breath to see if the Jedi Master could convince the little Padawan to take on Darth Vader, a man so large Oliver only came up to about his hip. The Jedi Master over-emphasized every move and did each one with Oliver.

Thankfully, Darth Vader had protection in specific places because Oliver's last hit was not to the routine and he gave Vader a whack in a sensitive place. The whole crowd was cheering Oliver on and after he was done with Vader, he turned toward the crowd, stopped, and gave us a look that said, "Yeah, I did that," before taking his place in line.

The academy ends with the Jedi Master giving each Padawan their diploma on stage. Oliver was toward the end of the line, but the Jedi Master had all the kids go before Oliver. Finally, he knelt down and spoke to him for a few moments, then gave Oliver a fist bump and his diploma. Oliver ran down the stage exclaiming, "I did it! I was scared, but I did it! I beat Darth Vader!"

As we were giving him hugs and congratulations, one of the stagehands walked over and excitedly asked, "Are you Oliver? Your Jedi Master was so proud of you for overcoming your fear and battling Darth Vader that he wanted you to have this." He gave Oliver a red lightsaber signed by none other than Darth Vader. Joe and I teared up at the excitement on his face. Oliver gave him a huge hug and we thanked him profusely. Seeing a complete stranger care enough about their job to help your child overcome a fear, avoid a regret, and help them battle Darth Vader, and then give them an autographed lightsaber? That is the kind of magic you only have at Disney. We will never forget that Jedi Master and the special attention and magic he gave our family.

How do you top a pep talk from a Jedi Master, battling Darth Vader, and a free lightsaber? Well, you don't, but we knew Fantasmic! would be a huge hit. For dinner we were lucky enough to grab a place in the Tune-In Lounge located next to the 50's Prime Time Cafe. This is an eclectically decorated space right off the restaurant that feels more like a room in your grandparent's house or sitting in a Technicolor episode of *Leave It to Beaver*. Reservations aren't required for the lounge, but getting a seat can be tricky. Most folks just come in to wait for their 50's Prime Time Cafe reservation, but we started a trend by taking a seat on a pastel-colored leather couch in front of an old black-and-white TV and enjoying a tray of comfort food right there in the lounge. Oliver munched on cheese, grapes, and a smoothie, while Joe and I shared the sampling of "Mom's Favorites." I'm a huge fan of homemade fried chicken, so crispy fried chicken with creamy mashed potatoes paired with one of Dad's shocking blue cocktails and I could have taken a nap right then. But, it was time to head to Fantasmic!

Fantasmic! is one of my favorite nighttime shows. Joe, Oliver, and I had great seats and enjoyed the pre-show entertainment from two goofy guys that split the stadium into two teams competing for noise, the ability to do the Wave, and Disney sing-a-longs. We were on Team Bear Tank and sadly lost to Team Awesome Mustache. Before the show started, we grabbed a big box of salty popcorn and the Just Goodies Dessert offering platter. The black platter included salty pretzel sticks covered in bittersweet chocolate, one with candies and the other with a drizzle of white chocolate and sprinkles. With a side of fluffy marshmallows and juicy red strawberries with a rich bittersweet chocolate sauce for dunking, this was a surprisingly tasty treat to have while sitting on concrete bleachers.

The show began and we were enthralled by projections from our favorite movies onto walls of water, ships full of princes and princesses, and Mickey's epic battle. When the snake appeared on the stage to attack Mickey, Oliver stood up and yelled "Mickey! Mickey! Look out!" The finale, when Mickey defeated the snake and goes from the battle to the top of the rocks in a blast of fireworks and appears in a sparkling suit, did Oliver in. He was so excited for Mickey and talked about it the rest of the night.

Day 3

This was the hottest day of the trip, and we spent it in Epcot, the largest of the Disney parks, and which can be a mixed bag when it's so hot and crowded. Because of World Showcase, however, it's our favorite park, and offers the most escapes from the heat, but sometimes you have to walk awhile to get there. A first for us was being at Epcot during the International Flower & Garden Festival. Entering the park we were greeted by topiary versions of Mickey, Minnie, Goofy, and other characters. Throughout the park there were exhibits, special merchandise, gorgeous landscapes, and the best part, for Oliver, playgrounds.

There was a whole section with plants and interactive play spaces resembling *The Wizard of Oz*. The display of flowers on the Future World side of the World Showcase Lagoon was stunning. The bright white, tangerine orange, and brilliant fuchsia plants were arranged in flower shapes that spread across the entire water's edge. The display was immense and was beautifully complimented by the clusters of flowers on floating displays in the water. In World Showcase, there was even a miniature train set with multiple miniature plantings. The level of detail was stunning—from hanging planters with bright pink flowers at the train station, to pots with purple and orange flowers outside a few of the miniature homes.

> **TIP!** If you have anyone in your life who loves gardening, take them to Epcot's International Flower & Garden. What the Disney landscape designers are able to do with flowers is stunning, and, because it's Disney, there is a playful side to the displays. It is also a great place for foodies because the Outdoor Kitchens feature tastes from around the world, many made with fresh garden ingredients. As a food lover, I feel as if I'm cheating on Food & Wine Festival, but I think I enjoyed

the food at Flower & Garden even more. It may have more to do with the shorter lines and smaller crowds, but there were a lot of very tasty bites at Flower & Garden.

Between two of the pavilions in World Showcase, we were in the right place at the right time and hit the character jackpot. They were entering from behind a magical gate that was set back from the main walkways, and no one was really noticing they were there. First came Max, Goofy's son. Oliver had his Yoda with him from the day before and he and Max had a blast playing with it. As the cast member went to take the photo, she yelled, "Do the Boba Fett stance." Oliver must have heard wrong and did his take on a Boba Fett *dance*. Max and the wrangler thought it was hysterical. Next was Gideon from *Pinocchio*. Oliver saw him and ran full force, giving him a huge hug—admitting afterwards, "Who was that? I just hugged him." Pinocchio came out and we got a great picture of him and Oliver holding hands and skipping together.

Then we saw him. The main man. The guy Oliver had talked non-stop about meeting. Mickey. He went running up and gave Mickey the biggest hug. Mickey messed around with Oliver's Yoda and then pretended to give him a cake with a candle and had Oliver blow it out when he saw the birthday button. Most people hadn't noticed yet he was there, so there wasn't a line and we could take our time. Donald was also there, but was being a bit standoffish and impatient. The cast member with him said Donald was being grumpy and Joe and I wondered what that meant. He's having a bad day or just needed a moment but was forced to go and get squeezed by small children? Either way, even grumpy Donald couldn't resist Oliver's big blue eyes, chubby cheeks, and birthday button, and they ended up dancing together. Oliver's character needs were totally sated for the day and it was one less line we had to stand in.

We had our lunch next to a huge topiary of Lightning McQueen, conveniently located next to a great playground where Oliver made a few new friends while Joe and I munched on treats from the Flower & Garden Outdoor Kitchens (otherwise known as food kiosks, similar to those at the Food & Wine Festival).

As Oliver played for almost an hour, Joe and I made quick trips to different kiosks. Each one focuses on a few different plantings. For lunch, we visited Florida Fresh and had the watermelon salad with red onions, baby arugula, feta cheese, and balsamic reduction. With the heat of the day this was a refreshing mix bursting with flavors of sweet watermelon, peppery arugula, and a salty bite from the Feta cheese. With the gentleness of the watermelon flavor, we felt the onions overpowered it a bit and the friendly cast member agreed and didn't add them on our second helping.

On the second trip we also tried the shrimp and stone ground grits with Andouille sausage, sweet corn, tomato, and cilantro. Another hit. The smooth creamy grits had whole kernels of corn that gave it a nice crunch. The shrimp on top was bursting with a bit of spiciness from the sausage and freshness of the tomato. Together in one bite it was an explosion of flavors with the sweet shrimp and sweet corn contrasting beautifully with the meatiness of the sausage and the brightness from the tomato and cilantro.

The most memorable bite was from the outdoor kitchen in France, where they offered a ratatouille tarte bursting with tomato and gently spiced vegetables, topped with goat cheese. The earthiness of the goat cheese with the rich tomato, bright bell peppers, and zucchini, with a bite from the eggplant on the buttery, flaky tart crust, gave you a different experience with each bite. Tomato, bell pepper, and goat cheese are flavors that I love together. Add in pastry and the fact that I love the movie *Ratatouille* and I was back for seconds, maybe even thirds. Joe and Oliver grabbed sweet treats at Les Halles Boulangerie Patisserie. Oliver had a fruit tart with multiple layers of pastry and fruit drizzled with a sugary glaze that he called a fruit burger.

After lunch, the Nemo ride provided a nice moment to cool down from the heat. Turtle Talk with Crush delivered a lot of laughs and Oliver even spotted a hidden Mickey in the fish tanks. Then we went on the Figment ride. When I was a little older than Oliver, I visited Disney World and fell in love with Figment. I even had a stuffed animal Figment that I dragged with me everywhere (it may still be in my mom's attic). I was thrilled to see Figment and the professor were back. Like Small World or Peter Pan's Flight, this ride is a tradition for me, but wow it has changed since what I remember as a kid. Figment is different and I didn't remember his voice being quite so annoying, especially when he is singing. Regardless, I loved reliving a moment from childhood, and because Joe and Oliver love me, they only complained a bit.

Next, we headed to dinner at Tutto Gusto Wine Cellar in the Italy pavilion. Epcot is jam-packed with amazing restaurants and knowing our little man's favorite meal is meats and cheeses, this was the perfect choice. We had a little table in front of a fireplace and a friendly waitress from Italy. This restaurant is a bit of a hidden gem, and provides a sanctuary from the heat with its brick walls and eclectic light fixtures. They kept the door open so you weren't blasted by the Florida air conditioning and the whole space felt like you were at a family restaurant in a little Italian village.

The food is small plates, our preferred way of eating, with a wide selection of meats and cheeses. We munched on salty, sweet prosciutto and finocchiniona—a salami flavored with fennel, black pepper, and creamy moist mozzarella. We even got Oliver to try some fruits of the sea with the insulate di mare that featured a delicious blend of shrimp, squid, and octopus, flavored with a brightness from the lemon and the earthiness of extra virgin olive oil. After sharing a generous helping of Nutella chocolate cake, we relaxed with a glass of Prosecco for me, an Italian craft beer for Joe, and a kiddie cocktail for Oliver.

Another first for us on this trip was testing out the Disney baby-sitting services. I booked the sitter over the phone and received a confirmation email and call when we arrived. They told me the name of the person who would be coming, a brief description of her, and the identification to request when she arrived. The sitters check in at the front desk, and then the front desk calls up to let you know they has arrived. Our sitter's name was Eleanor. She had the feel of a grandma who had helped raise a number of children and knew how to deal with adorable but strong-willed five-year-old boys. Eleanor had a number of rules including no going on the balcony. She and Oliver ended up getting along quite well because of their shared love of reading and spent most of the evening pouring over books she had brought with her.

While Oliver and Eleanor bonded over books, Joe and I headed over to the Wave at the Contemporary for a drink and a little nosh. True to its oceanic name, the Wave features an abundance of blue lighting, wave-like patterns on the walls, and furnishings with a contemporary vibe. The lounge has a bar area with the typical TV screens showing multiple sports so Joe and I chose to check out an area just off the bar that was aglow in the bright blue signature lights. My cocktail was blue and blended right in with the decor. The people-watching at the lounge was interesting, to say the least. There was a raucous group of couples that were downing shots with their cocktails, and a giggling group of women in their 20s that we suspected were part of a bachelorette party. Joe and I shared a few snacks and reminisced about the trip, thinking about the next time we would come—for our 10-year anniversary in 2015. As we were heading back to the room, we stopped by the gift shop at the Contemporary to get a few birthday surprises for Oliver and souvenirs for the other kids and my dad. We unknowingly timed it perfectly and crossed the bridge between the two hotels right as the fireworks lit the sky above Cinderella Castle. You can have a bit of romance on a family trip to Disney World.

CHAPTER TWELVE
Bugs Under My Butt and Lazy Susan

Day 4

Day four dawned nice and sunny as we headed on the bus to a character breakfast at Tusker House at Animal Kingdom. At Tusker House the characters are all in safari wear, even down to Minnie and Daisy's heels in an African wildlife-friendly khaki. Like most character breakfasts, there are a lot of people and the dining room is big and quite loud. It's not my favorite experience, but going to the early breakfast at Tusker House means early admission into the park and hopping on Kilimanjaro Safaris early enough in the day that it's still cool enough for the animals to be active.

Today was another big Oliver first: Mickey Waffles. These waffles were a huge source of anticipation as both Nate and Annie had him hyped about them. The breakfast featured a gigantic buffet with all the typical breakfast offerings: seasoned breakfast potatoes and crispy bacon that was quite tasty when dipped in the syrup around the Mickey Waffle. I timed it perfectly and they just brought out a new tray of Mickey Waffles so the outside was crispy and the inside soft and not too sweet. Timing is also key with the blintzes. With fresh blintzes, the puff pastry is crunchy and the inside is warm and cheesy with the sweet tartness of the cherries.

With its Animal Kingdom location, Tusker House offers a few treats not seen at most other Disney buffets like Basmati rice and sweet potato casserole. This was also Oliver's first time trying plantains, but it was really all about the Mickey Waffle. For this meal, Goofy, Daisy, Minnie, and Mickey walk around the dining room while Donald greets folks outside. Each character signed Oliver's poster and gave him birthday pats on the head.

After breakfast we headed over to Kilimanjaro Safaris. This was a huge hit with Oliver: "I saw a rhino really close up and a baby elephant. It was so cute. Huge but cute." After the ride, as we were crossing the bridge between lands, we came across a musician playing an instrument that resembled a xylophone. This was the first of a number of happy birthday songs for

Oliver. It was really very sweet and the man seemed almost excited to be able to sing it.

Next, we went to the Tree of Life and It's Tough to Be a Bug. I'm not a big fan of bugs, so this is one of my least favorites, but Oliver loved it and "liked the end with the bugs under my butt!"

Our next stop was Yak & Yeti Restaurant in Asia. Yak & Yeti is exotic, with dark carved furniture, beautiful artwork, Asian sculptures, and colorful Tibetan prayer flags scattered about. We feasted on the steamed pork buns. These are little nuggets of deliciousness. The inside is sweet barbecued pork that is surrounded by a soft white bun, almost like tasty Wonder bread. The buns are steamed and the bread gets soft and flavored by the meaty pork and tangy barbecue sauce.

The one disappointment of this day was that Oliver wasn't able to see the tigers at Maharajah Jungle Trek. It was typical Florida weather—one minute sunny, then a downpour. By the time we got the ponchos purchased and on, the rain was over. Ponchos are one of those purchases I have mixed feelings about. Spending hours walking around with wet underwear is not anyone's idea of fun, but paying $10 for a piece of plastic that you will likely use for about 10 minutes isn't either. Every time we just about made it to the Maharajah Jungle Trek the weather changed again and the trail closed. After three tries, we gave up.

Oliver was disappointed until we came across a habitat of gibbons. One benefit of the rain is the animals all become very active. There was one tiny baby gibbon that was hanging from its mom while she was swinging from ropes near the very tops of the trees. This, and the excitement of playing on the dinosaur playground, ensured that the tigers were quickly forgotten.

Once again I made a fool of myself on the DINOSAUR ride. Oliver covered his ears for most of it, but really loved the bouncy wild trip back in time and seeing all the different dinosaurs. He insisted that we purchase the DINOSAUR ride pic to show how silly Mama looked.

TIP! Animal Kingdom is a great park that always seems to be the last on many guests' lists. I've had more than one person tell me, "I've been to a zoo." Calling Animal Kingdom a zoo is like calling Buckingham Palace a house. At the time of publication, Disney is about to open Rivers of Light, a new nighttime show at Animal Kingdom. Having stayed at Kidani Village at Animal Kingdom Lodge and seeing how active the animals are at dusk, I can promise that being at Animal Kingdom at night will be a real adventure. The park is absolutely worth the visit. You can slow down and just stroll and take in the sights, the smells, and the unique tastes, then scream your head off on Expedition Everest. Disney is constantly adding attractions to the park and Rivers of Light looks like it will give Wishes at Magic Kingdom and Fantasmic! at Hollywood Studios some competition.

After purchasing a few more character packs, a fancy rock for Austin at the shop in DinoLand U.S.A, and a funny t-shirt featuring a sad T-Rex with the phrase ,"If you're happy and you know it clap your...oh," we headed back to Bay Lake to get ready for Oliver's birthday dinner at Whispering Canyon Cafe in Wilderness Lodge. When I called Disney Dining to make reservations for this trip, I asked about a restaurant for boys' birthdays, and the agent recommended Whispering Canyon Café, hands down. We got to take our first boat ride of the trip to go from Bay Lake over to Wilderness Lodge. The dock is right outside the Contemporary, about a 5-minute walk from Bay Lake Tower. The boats are beautiful, classic looking crafts operated by friendly skippers in traditional captain's costumes. Unlike the boats you take from Hollywood Studios to Beach Club or from Magic Kingdom to Polynesian, this boat looked like something straight out of a 1920s movie. It was much smaller and gave us a more intimate, enjoyable ride.

As we rode along the lake, it was if we were transported to a wilder country. The trees were thicker and the architecture of Wilderness Lodge stood in stark contrast to the modern Contemporary. When arriving at Wilderness Lodge by lake, the first thing you see is the huge pool with the cave and a slide. There are long piers and wooden walkaways along the front and the lodge itself towers in the background looking like a gigantic, luxurious log cabin. Walking up to the hotel is a treat, because there are birds singing all around and the walkways are large and meander through the trees. Benches are thoughtfully placed, and as you near the hotel there are rocking chairs if you need a moment to catch your breath. There are huge multi-story windows and you can see the beams along the ceiling and the thick wooden columns supporting the high roof. Once inside there are totem poles featuring Disney characters, more comfy rocking chairs, multi-story fireplaces, and balconies stories high, leading to the guest rooms.

TIP! Call Disney Dining at some point during your planning. Yes, it is much easier and faster to book online, but there is nothing like getting a passionate Disney enthusiast to help you book your dining reservations. If it weren't for the amazing folks at Disney Dining I would never have learned about Whispering Canyon Cafe at Wilderness Lodge, watching Magic Kingdom fireworks from the beach outside Polynesian, the exotic and delicious Sanaa at Animal Kingdom Lodge, and the Fantasmic! dinner package. These cast members really know their Disney munchies and will often-even help with tips on how to get tricky reservations, like Be Our Guest at Magic Kingdom.

You can hear Whispering Canyon Cafe before you see it. There is a lot of whooping and hollering and smells of barbecue chicken. The waiting area has a huge wooden LEGO table that Joe and Oliver jumped right on. The cafe is a sprawling place. If you don't mind the noise and want to be part of the action, ask if you can be in the main dining room. Behind the dining room, to the side of the kitchen, is a space with a few smaller tables near a fireplace. Further beyond that are a few tables that run along the back of the restaurant and are situated in an area that resembles the front porch of a country house.

After we were seated, a short, friendly woman came over and introduced herself as Lazy Susan. Upon hearing it was the day before Oliver's 5th birthday and seeing his button she began to use the surprisingly loud voice contained in her small frame. We ordered a family meal with BBQ meats, baked beans, corn bread, and potatoes. Oliver once again went for a grilled cheese.

Next thing we heard is a request for all of the dads to come into the main dining room. Being the good sport that he is (and with some pleading from his chubby-cheeked birthday boy), Joe headed into the main room with us. All of the dads stood in a half circle at the front of the dining room and were instructed how to perform the Little Teapot dance. Then the entire dining room, and a crowd that had gathered in the lobby, were serenaded by an array of dads. They received a standing ovation. Next, there was a fake horse race with all the kids dashing around the restaurant. It was a great idea because many of the kids were over-excited after watching their dads performance.

By this time, Lazy Susan and Oliver had bonded, and our food was there. Oliver has a bit of Dug (the dog from *Up*) syndrome. He's easily distracted, especially when it's time to eat. After 30 minutes with the food, he had maybe eaten half his sandwich. So, while we were making a birthday video for my brother, whose birthday was that day, Lazy Susan came barreling into the dining room hollering "Oliver" at the top of her lungs and telling him to eat. Oliver jumped and then cracked up and Lazy Susan looked a bit embarrassed about her boisterous appearance on our video call.

Next was the birthday boy's cupcake and Lazy Susan demanding all the folks in our section, including this cute young couple who were unsuccessfully trying to have a romantic dinner, sing him "Happy Birthday." When this couple asked Susan to take a picture of them in front of the fireplace, she invited Oliver into the photo. Oliver described it best, "Susan yelled my name during our video for Uncle Miah and then had me get a picture with these people I didn't know. They even sang "Happy Birthday" to me. Susan made me laugh, but she was crazy!"

CHAPTER THIRTEEN
Celebrating 5 Years of Oliver

Day 5

Today was the big day. The birthday. It all started with a voicemail from Mickey saying happy birthday, which caused a huge smile and giggles. This is another one of those Disney moments that may seem just a small thing for Disney to do, just a voicemail, but it makes your child feel special. It's that small touch that makes it all the more magical for them. We also received an envelope under our door that was a birthday card with the autographs of the Fab Five characters. We packed up our backpack and stroller and walked over to the Magic Kingdom.

The birthday breakfast was a cinnamon roll the size of Oliver's head with a LeFou's Brew and a side of pork shank from Gaston's in Fantasyland. Joe and Oliver love their sweets and this cinnamon roll was lathered in white creamy frosting and was gigantic. I'm more a savory girl, especially at breakfast, so I sat there feeling like a caveman gnawing on the meaty, also quite huge but nicely seasoned pork shank. Gaston's is perfectly themed. In the dining room you feel as if you have been transported into the movie with the oversized wooden chairs and tables and large fireplace with the portrait of Gaston above the mantel. Outside the windows you can see the fountain where Belle enjoyed her books and a series of small buildings with cobblestone walkways. It's a picturesque corner of Fantasyland not to be missed. We hit all the Fantasyland favorites, attending PhilHarmagic three times and going on Peter Pan's Flight twice.

Peter Pan's Flight is one of those classic Disney rides that is a must-do each visit. As you are soaring through the darkness in your ship, you feel like you are peeking in at a glowing version of many of the key scenes from the film. My favorite part is zig-zagging up the Thames with Big Ben and London glowing beneath you. Coming eye to eye with Captain Hook while he tries to save himself from the alligator's snapping jaws was Oliver's favorite thing of the day.

After a spin under the sea on Ariel's Undersea Adventure, we tried but failed to get into Be Our Guest. The line was over 2.5 hours long and stretched from inside the building to the walkway before the bridge. It was Mother's Day and Be Our Guest was the place to be. So we headed over to Haunted Mansion, then the first of two rides on Big Thunder Mountain, and one more go on Pirates.

Then we made one of our best decisions and went back to the hotel for a dip in the pool. This was Oliver's first ride down a big water slide by himself. The pool at Bay Lake, like most Disney pools, is great for smaller kids because there are two different slides, a splash area, and a gradual entry. Joe is not a big swimmer, so while he sat in the shade reading, Oliver and I ran up and down the ramp, went down the slides, and chased each other through the splash area. Lunch was a few snacks by the pool with a box of Cinnamon Toast Crunch in the room.

We headed back into the park to watch SpectroMagic, Celebrate the Magic, and Wishes from Main Street. Just because it's fun, we walked over to the Contemporary and took the monorail the long way over to Magic Kingdom. After a nighttime ride on Big Thunder and a few of Oliver's other favorites, we hit the stores along Main Street before the shows began.

As we were getting some salty popcorn from somewhere in Belle's village, we noticed crowds of folks staking places behind the castle. I've read in a few places about viewing the fireworks from this angle where you can see them over three castles: Cinderella's, Beast's, and Prince Eric's. Since this was Oliver's first time really seeing the fireworks, we headed over to Main Street near the bridge to Tomorrowland and scored a great location right near a closed ice cream cart where we could rest our feet by sitting on the rail.

> **TIP!** The best place to watch Celebrate the Magic and the fireworks in comfort is to do the FastPass+ or the Wishes Dessert Party. Being able to have space to spread out and sit down during the nighttime shows is incredible. When the park is busy, this will offer the best and most comfortable view, especially if you have been battling the crowds all day. You miss out on the photo op of your kid on Dad or Grandpa's shoulders, but their backs will thank you. And it never failed that we would end up stuck behind the family of professional basketball players.

Oliver has a mixed relationship with fireworks. Sometimes he loves them, but there have been other times when the loud noise freaks him out. On this night, the Disney magic must have been working because he loved every second. SpectroMagic, the nighttime parade featuring floats and characters decked out in twinkle lights, ended up being the first parade that we saw from beginning to end on the whole trip. Oliver especially loved seeing Hook's ship all lit up with Peter Pan and Hook sparking in bright lights.

Then it was time for Celebrate the Magic. It's even more amazing from inside the park. This is my favorite part of the nighttime show. The way they transform the castle from looking like a Scottish castle from *Brave* to the stained glass from *Beauty and the Beast* to the Cheshire Cat is truly magical. We had just seen the movie *Wreck-It Ralph*, so when Oliver saw that part he starting yelling "Guys! Guys! Mama, Dada, Ralph's wrecking the castle!" This resulted in us making a new friend with a cast member who was in the college program and there all the way from Australia.

The bridge near Tomorrowland was a brilliant location for Celebrate the Magic and good for the fireworks. Despite it being Mother's Day and perfect weather, the crowd levels were surprisingly low. Overall, we had beautiful weather this trip and manageable crowd levels. I've heard earlier in May you get more rain and cloudy days, but we were lucky and the sky was clear this night. The fireworks lit up the sky, little kids sang about wishes, and I squeezed Joe's hand while my birthday boy whispered, "Wow! Best birthday ever!"

CHAPTER FOURTEEN
Not-So-Evil Stepmother
Disney Secret #4

10 Tips for Fitting It All In

Keeping your group sane, energized, and enjoying themselves can be tricky. Disney can be like trying to sprint a marathon. Solution? Prepare yourself mentally and follow these 10 tips.

Tip 1: Ask everyone for their top three attractions/things to see/places to eat. Their picks might surprise you. In 2005, for Austin, it was the pool, Space Mountain, and Tower of Terror. Ten years later that list was the pool, time for shopping for gifts, and going to Universal, which is why I always warn that I cannot guarantee we will do everything on the list.

Tip 2: Prioritize. For each park, create A and B lists for the attractions, shows, and restaurants. A's are must sees, B's are the ones you want to do, but can live without. Everything cannot be an A and there will be some attractions and shows that won't make either list. Your FastPasses should definitely include as many A's as possible. So, if you have a group with a broad range of ages, your lists for Magic Kingdom might be:

- *A List*: Seven Dwarfs Mine Train, Mickey's PhilharMagic, Buzz Lightyear's Space Ranger Spin, Space Mountain, Big Thunder Mountain Railroad, Haunted Mansion, Peter Pan's Flight, Pirates of the Caribbean, Wishes.

- *B List*: Tomorrowland Transit Authority PeopleMover, Mad Tea Party, Casey Jr's Splash and Soak Station, Dumbo the Flying Elephant, Barnstormer, Journey of the Little Mermaid, Enchanted Tales with Belle, Tigger Character Spot, Gaston's.

Tip 3: Figure out which parks you should visit more than once—for us, it's always Magic Kingdom because of the number of attractions and we *have* to see Celebrate the Magic and Wishes. In 2015, we added Epcot as a park we should visit more than once because of the Food & Wine Festival.

Tip 4: Use FastPass+ for events. Now this is a tricky decision because FastPass+ work like this. You can pre-book three per day. You can book another FP+ once you have used your three. So, if you book a nighttime show, you will probably not be able to use more than three FP+ that day. However, nighttime shows at all the parks are big events and draw huge crowds. Just think, on an average day Magic Kingdom has 53,000 guests. That may not seem like much when they're spread out over 107 acres, 40 attractions, and many shops and restaurants. But come nighttime at least 10,000 of these guests want to watch the fireworks just like you. So they all try to squeeze themselves into about 10 acres of that 107 to have a good view of the show.

Save your feet, the claustrophobics in your group, and your sanity—book yourself a designated space to watch the show. I recommend this for the nighttime shows at Magic Kingdom and, as seating is limited for the new Rivers of Light at Animal Kingdom, it would be wise there as well. If you are in Disney World during low crowd levels, maybe forgo using a FastPass for Illuminations (Epcot's nighttime fireworks show) or Fantasmic! at Hollywood Studios. Illuminations and Fantasmic! both offer dinner packages with reserved seating for the nighttime shows, and Magic Kingdom has a Wishes Dessert Party.

Tip 5: Book your FastPass+ for attractions wisely. There are some rides that really do require a FP+, but there are others that have lines typically not long enough to justify it. Be realistic in your expectations. If its 4 p.m. and you want to book a FP+ for Seven Dwarfs Mine Train, you're probably out of luck. Here are the FP+ we would absolutely book again, by park.

At the Magic Kingdom, book Wishes. The FP+ we booked for Wishes will go down as one of our best Disney decisions ever. Next, Seven Dwarfs Mine Train. I have heard that the theming in this line is pretty cool but with wait times at 70 minutes only 20 minutes after the park opens, it's a FP+ worth using. Both Big Thunder Mountain and Space Mountain are rides that have experienced increased wait times since the creation of FP+, so if you want to experience these, a FP+ is worth it, especially if you are there during the warm months. Big Thunder Mountain's lines can get pretty warm. Peter Pan's Flight is another to consider.

Now you may have noticed that I'm well above the 3 FP+ per day that you can pre-book; it's just one more reason why we always schedule more than one day at Magic Kingdom. There are a few attractions that probably don't need a FastPass unless you have limited time, the park is super busy, or you *must* experience a certain attraction. They include Mickey's PhilharMagic because it's in a theatre and even with FP+, you will likely only ever have to wait through one show; Dumbo has a super fun circus waiting area where you can cool off, rest your feet, and get a pager to use for your ride time; and Voyage of the Little Mermaid has a fun line that's out of the heat and actually very cool to be in at night.

Both Epcot and Hollywood Studios have tiered FastPass booking systems. Basically, the tiered system means you can't book all the most popular attractions because you can only book one Tier 1 FastPass. At Epcot, Soarin' should definitely be on the list. If you want to have any shot of meeting Anna and Elsa, go with that. Test Track and Mission: SPACE are others to consider because the lines can get very long. The Seas with Nemo & Friends is a good one, but the line is primarily inside so can be skipped if you have another high priority. If the park is very busy and you are set on Illuminations, it may be worth it, but I'd recommend doing the Illuminations dinner package if you only have one day at Epcot and want to hit the three most popular rides (Soarin', Mission: SPACE, and Test Track). Spaceship Earth has a pretty fast moving line so don't use up a perfectly good FastPass on that. You can also catch it on your way out of the park to rest your feet before the walk to your room or car.

At Hollywood Studios, if Toy Story Mania is on your list, book the FastPass. The lines get very long very quickly and this can be a difficult attraction to experience with anything less than a 50-minute wait unless you sprint to the ride at dawn and take out any grandmas that get in your way. Tower of Terror is one of our group's favorite attractions in Hollywood Studios and is in the top 10 for all of Disney World. If it's an absolute must and you don't want a line, add it to your FP+ list. Depending on your group, the Frozen Sing-Along may be a good one to add as it's not a Tier 1. If Rock 'n' Roller Coaster is on your list, book all your FP+ for the morning and once you've used them, try to get one for Rock 'n' Roller Coaster. If you're not doing the Fantasmic! dining package and Fantasmic! is a must see, book that after you have used the rest of your FastPasses. Don't waste your FP+ on Muppet*Vision 3D as it's in a large theatre with plenty of seats. I'd also hold off on Star Tours unless it's Star Wars Weekend or very crowded because that line moves fairly quickly, is either shaded or indoors, and has some fun things to see.

Animal Kingdom has a lot of shows that are worth FP+. The shows aren't really our thing, but I have heard Nemo and the Lion King are must-sees. Kilimanjaro Safaris should absolutely be on your list. Try to get this FP+ in the morning or as late in the day as possible, since the animals are much more active when it's cooler. Expedition Everest is another must, but the line is pretty fun and moves quickly so you can save that FP+ and plan to wait in line. DINOSAUR is another to consider, though its line moves fairly quickly, is primarily indoors, and is typically under 30 minutes unless the park is *very* busy. I wouldn't recommend using your FP+ on Tough to Be a Bug or the Primeval Whirl unless they are A-list priority for you, the park is super busy, or you nothing else to do. Both have reasonably fast lines and Tough to Be a Bug has a fun waiting area; we've never had to wait longer than 20 minutes for it.

Tip 6: Make dining reservations for events. There are options for many of the nightly shows at the four parks. All of them offer a great opportunity to ensure you either have a place to sit or that you have one of the best views in the house. Make sure the Fantasmic! dinner package is on your list. The IllumiNations dinner package around the holidays gets you a seat at the Candlelight Processional and a great view for the holiday fireworks afterward. At the Magic Kingdom, there is a dessert party in Tomorrowland, but I recommend doing the Wishes FP+ instead and bringing some tasty treats from Casey's or Main Street Confectionery.

Tip 7: Eat a good lunch, or graze. With grandparents, college students, and kids used to eating on a set schedule, it's important to make sure everyone is getting enough to eat and drink. There are few things worse than getting hungry in Disney World. Disney has been working hard to make munching even more magical at counter-service locations. Check out curry dogs at Harambe Market at Animal Kingdom, fried shrimp or the lobster roll at Columbia Harbour House in Magic Kingdom, Mediterranean falafel wrap at Tangierine Café in the Morocco pavilion, tartine aux fromages from Les Halles Boulangerie Patisserie in the France pavilion, macaroni and cheese with pulled pork at Min and Bill's Dockside Diner in Hollywood Studios, or a quick Mickey ice cream just about anywhere.

Tip 8: Try to get into Be Our Guest—the hardest and most worthwhile reservation. The food and surroundings are both magical and will be among the most unforgettable moments from your trip.

Tip 9: Make dining part of the experience. From belly dancers to drive-in movies to eating in an aquarium or dining in a castle with princesses, Disney theming is not limited to rides and shows. Disney realizes that eating is part of the experience and offers many ways to taste something new. Most people will schedule a character meal and I recommend you do it for breakfast, but character meals just scratch the surface of what Disney has to offer. Try something new: sit in the ballroom from *Beauty and the Beast* (Be Our Guest), eat comfort food in a 1950's kitchen (50's Prime Time Café), share some nachos under a dark sky in a Mayan temple (San Angel Inn), sample dim sum while admiring artifacts from the Himalayas (Yak & Yeti), or savor butter chicken while a giraffe walks by (Sanaa).

Tip 10: With over 2.9 million shirts and 2.5 million pairs of Mickey ears sold ever year in Disney World alone, shopping is part of the magic for most guests. Every year Disney creates a line of merchandise branded for that year. With t-shirts, pins, stationary, photo frames and albums, bags, pencils, stuffed animals, and even ears, this line include scores of new items annually. Add this to the merchandise featuring new characters or related to a film release and the hordes of stuff that the Disney merchandising geniuses think up to get you to scan that MagicBand. Shopping can be its own theme park.

CHAPTER FIFTEEN
Not-So-Evil Stepmother
Disney Secret #5

. . . .

Packing for the Magic

I'm not as vain as the Evil Queen nor am I planning to poison my wonderful bonus daughters, but I do like to look good, even when we are on a vacation that involves walking about 10 miles a day. Within our group, Nick and Austin are the only ones who don't care that much. Austin just wanted to make sure he had a photo at Disney in his co-ed cheerleading shirt. For the rest of us, it requires planning. Sam, Annie, and Mags were all into DisneyBounding (dressing up in contemporary versions of your favorite Disney characters) and had been gathering hairstyle photos, vintage t-shirts, and comfy flats for months. Nate was all about his t-shirts and even had a few picked for specific parks. My dad is the same way and had his "¡Por favor manténgase alejado de las puertas!" t-shirt for our monorail day. Joe's version of casual is linen pants and lightweight button-down shirts, and all Oliver cared about was being around Nate as much as possible, and that he had his Jedi Academy t-shirt. Shoes are always a bit of a challenge for me, but I have found that a good pair of espadrilles is invaluable. I planned for what I would pack months in advance, did a few fashion shows for Joe, and didn't try to poison beautiful Annie once.

Stock up on travel-size toiletries. For face creams, special lotions, and those tricky products that don't come in travel size, pick up a set of travel bottles. Use the Ziploc space of the low-maintenance men in your life. I always use that space to pack things like shampoo and sunscreen, as it's easy to justify because everyone uses them. Make a pit stop on your way from the airport and have a list. Quite a few of the car services will make a stop for you at a grocery store or a Walgreens/CVS. The cost savings of purchasing toiletries, breakfast and snack foods, and bottled drinks outside the Disney "bubble" instead of on-site at your hotel can go a long way to paying for the cost of the hired car. There are also a few grocery services that deliver to Disney resorts.

Standing in baggage claim is a waste of perfectly good park time, so we try and travel carry-on only. The most important trick to carry-on only is planning and being willing to tell yourself no. You will likely have to wear a shirt or maybe a pair of pants or sweatshirt more than once. I also do a lot of layers on the flight out, sometimes having 2 days worth of shirts on, and plan it so some shirts I end up wearing as pajamas or for lounging in later. This also requires knowing when you have too many clothes. You will not need 3 pairs of sneakers, your 2 super-cute black dresses, 12 pairs of underwear, or two bulky sweaters at Disney (unless you are going late November through February; it can get surprisingly chilly at night).

If you know where you are eating, the parks you are visiting, and where you can expect Florida air conditioning, you can plan out your wardrobe and fit at least 7 days in the largest United/American-approved carry-on. If you are staying at a villa, you can (usually) do laundry in the room and most of the Disney hotels have a self-laundry on site. We were able to have every person in our group of 11 do carry-on only, including me with my shoe obsession and Annie, the girl who once had a bag just for shoes. Sam and Nate were able to share a single carry-on bag, so we had one whole empty bag for souvenirs on the way home. I promise you, it can be done.

Whether you decide to do carry-on only or not, make sure everyone has a change of clothes in their carry-on in case the room isn't ready. In the last 10 years, my room was ready twice and once was on a work trip and I arrived late. The last thing you want is to be starving, tired, and trying to dig through your well-packed suitcase trying to figure out what to wear on 4 hours sleep. Have a pre-set outfit ready to go for each member of your party easily accessible in their carry-on. Also, have your in-the-park bag packed up when you leave the house. Then, when it's a 3-hour wait for your room, you can pop in the pool bathrooms (they usually have great changing spaces), change, freshen up, give your bags to the bellman, and be on your way.

Carrying supplies in the park is tricky. For most of our trips, we have had either a backpack or stroller. Annie, Sam, and Maggie all had small purses, but with the Magic Bands you really only need to carry the essentials. By the last few days of the trip, you find that most of the things you have been lugging around for days, you can live without. Here are a just a few things to consider carrying in the parks:

- Phone charger and charging pack. It's heavy, so only do this on the days when you are not able to make it back to your room or don't want to fight the crowds at the limited number of charging stations in the parks.

- Long-sleeve shirts for everyone. Never forget the Florida air conditioning in restaurants and even some ride lines can be arctic.

- Towel, for when you have to sit on the ground, especially during fireworks and parades.

- Ziploc bags. They are great for keeping Disney pins and their backs together, holding extras from the sometimes large Disney food portions, and because you never know.

- Journal for you or the kids. Phones are great, but I'm old-fashioned and loved having the ability to interview everyone and write it down.

- Bottle of water. Disney is surprisingly great about letting guest refill water bottles.

- Snacks like pretzels, crackers, and packs of cereal. It's an easy way to save money because those snacks can add up and it's also great for low blood sugar or an upset stomach.

- Tums, headache medicine, and travel-size sunscreen.

- If you have smaller children, a change of clothes, especially at Magic Kingdom where there are water play areas. This way you won't hear whining about walking around in wet underpants.

If you listen to no other tips, please listen to this one: if you have a baby that is big enough or a child under the age of 6 that is small enough, bring your own umbrella stroller. Some folks rent strollers from Disney, which is just one more line, is not cheap, and isn't guaranteed—occasionally, they do run out. Also, trying to find your stroller in the sea of Disney strollers is like *Where's Waldo* at the striped-shirt convention. And, Disney strollers can't leave the parks. Your long walk to the car or hotel room is even longer with a 40-pound 4-year-old. Other folks rent from a service, which again is not cheap and then you are lugging the stroller everywhere for your whole trip. The umbrella stroller easily folds away for riding the monorail and the buses, and it can hold its own in stroller parking. If you're flying it can also make the walk from the terminal to your gate much faster. Find one with a bottom storage section and now you have a place for those last-minute souvenirs. For Oliver, we attached his backpack to the bars and were able to keep all the 5-year-old-in-a-theme-park supplies: water, sunscreen, extra shorts, shirt and underwear, towel, *Guide to the Magic for Kids* journal, snacks like little boxes of cereal, and a stuffed animal for when he passed out cold as we were walking.

Experience 2015: Disney for 11

Well, I see no reason why you can't go…if you get all your work done.
—Lady Tremaine, *Cinderella*

CHAPTER SIXTEEN
Food, Family, and Giraffes!

By this time in our life, the hardest part of the trip was trying to find a week that our entire clan of 11 would all be able to take the same time off from work, school, and other responsibilities.

Cast

Ten years later and we have gone from a party of eight to a group of eleven:

- Dad (Bob), also known as Grandpa, and still the man behind the camera, but this time with higher-tech equipment, and in many more pictures himself thanks to PhotoPass photographers. This was his fourth trip to Disney World

- Mom (Debbie), also known as Grandma. Ten years and three grandkids later, still the thrill seeker. This was her fourth trip to Disney World.

- Joe, also known as Dad, Dada, and Bonus Dad. This was his sixth trip to Disney.

- Me, also known as Mom and Bonus Mom (it just sounds nicer than "step-mom"). This was my first Food & Wine Festival, and my eighth trip to Disney World.

- Nate, aged 26 and probably the second most excited of the group (after Sam). This was his fourth trip to Disney World.

- Maggie/Mags, aged 23 and still an avid writer, but now with a college writing degree behind it. Maggie and I were both tied to our notebooks jotting down notes and ideas. She was the one who taught me about DisneyBounding. This was her third trip to Disney World.

- Annie/Ann, aged 18 and still determined to find Tigger, but now in her freshman year of college. This was her third trip to Disney World.

- Austin/Stin, aged 15 and a sophomore in high school. This was his ninth trip to Disney World.

- Oliver, aged seven and for the first time with all his siblings on a Disney trip. This was his second trip to Disney World.

- Samantha (Sam), aged 26 and Nate's long-term girlfriend (they started dating right around our wedding in 2005). This was her second trip to Disney World.
- Nick, aged 20 and Annie's boyfriend. This was his fifth trip to Disney World.

Itinerary

- *Day 1*. We depart on an early flight Sunday October 11, 2015, in time for lunch at Sanaa and then right over to Magic Kingdom.
- *Day 2*: Epcot and the Food & Wine Festival
- *Day 3*: Hollywood Studios, with lunch at Sci-Fi Dine-In Theater.
- *Day 4*: A free day, spent park hopping between Hollywood Studios, Epcot, and Magic Kingdom.
- *Day 5*: Animal Kingdom, with lunch at Yak & Yeti and an anniversary dinner at Jiko.
- *Day 6*: Magic Kingdom, with lunch at Be Our Guest and then dinner at Kona Cafe in the Polynesian.
- *Day 7*. We pack, have lunch at Sanaa, and then head home.

When booking this trip I had my heart set on the Beach Club Villas. We loved the location so much and wanted to stick with what we knew. And then reality set in. No Beach Club. Alright, Bay Lake Tower then. Sorry, but no. Okay, how about the villas at the Polynesian? Nope.

"This is one of our busiest times of year, so it's difficult to get a reservation," said the cast member in reservations. "Since you have nine people there are only a few options that have two-bedroom villas that can accommodate nine. So we would need to look at one of those or a three-bedroom villa. I have a three-bedroom at Old Key West or a two-bedroom at Kidani Village, or I can offer the bungalows at the Polynesian, but you would need two and that would be a total cost of $40,000."

This was the first trip ever I wasn't able to get the hotel I wanted. The type-A planner in me was a bit crushed. So it was either completely blow the budget (not a viable option) or stay at a non-park hotel that, though the reviews were great, didn't have a ton of appeal for. We chose the option with the animals and our whole group—even my parents, who didn't stay at the same hotel but did come over to check out our animal menagerie— were thrilled with the choice.

TIP! Have a list of your top five Disney resorts and if you're going during a busy time, don't have your heart set on any of them. Do some research before calling Disney to book your reservation. The agents are typically helpful in recommending hotels based on your needs, but it is worth taking 10 minutes or so to check out pro/con lists on one of the many Disney websites. After staying in a number of different resorts, I've learned a thing or two about what to ask yourself to help you decide what hotel is right for your group.

Packing for this trip was one of the many pre-trip activities I savored. This is one of those times I can be a bit too military-like because I strongly suggested to everyone that they plan ahead, pack at least a few days in advance of the trip, and that they have to do it carry-on only. A trip to Disney requires packing planning. I want to look good on a Disney trip, but know that the last time I walked this much was our last trip to Disney, so shoes were key.

And then it was here! The night before a Disney vacation is filled with much anticipation. You feel like there is still a lot to do, but it's mostly done. Now it's just a matter of getting there.

Each of us had what I call "amusement bags" that went under their seats on the plane. Oliver's was filled with books and a few action figures so all the boys could play "fighting guys." Maggie had her notebook and Sam her sketchbook, Bob his camera, and Mom and Joe had their iPads. For the older kids, it was primarily phones and Nintendo 3DSs that got them through the plane ride. My Mickey and Minnie pins were joined by my Disney Pook-A-Loc journal (for taking all the notes for this book), a laptop for making and changing reservations, a 3 oz. bag, socks for going through security, and an iPad loaded with Disney books.

TIP! Four-roller suitcase. I remember the time where just two rollers was the luxury or when you would see people schlepping all their bags through the airport. Now there is the amazing four-roller. I have traveled a lot for work and swear by the Dash suitcase from Brookstone. The case is hard-sided and comes in a variety of colors, so if you have to end up checking your bag, your stuff is safe and, with the right color, easy to find in baggage claim. You can even put your other carry-ons on top and if there is a lack of seating, it can even work as a chair. Get the red one with a Mickey luggage tag and you are DisneyBounding!

CHAPTER SEVENTEEN
Traveling to a Small World

Day 1

We are leaving! We had to wake up at 3 a.m. with a car leaving at 3:30 a.m. When I'm traveling with a group, airports stress me out. I used to travel quite a bit for work, often internationally, and had my routine pretty much down, so I was rarely stressed or nervous. But when I'm traveling with the family, I always get nervous about missing the flight, getting stuck in the security line, losing our seats, not having enough overhead space for our bags, basically everything. Between the fees, standing at the airport waiting for bags, and the worry of "will my bag get there," my preference is to just do it all in carry-ons.

For me, the best mornings involve Starbucks, so we made a pit stop on the way to the gate to stock up on lattes, frappuccino's, and a smoothie for Oliver. We got great pics at the airport. Sam, the resident artist, was even doing some sketching of the people, bags, and various electronics. You can see the excitement on everyone's face, but also the exhaustion. Bob and Joe were able to sleep on the plane. We saw the most beautiful sunrise as we were flying toward Florida—all deep oranges and reds with a hint of pink. It felt like a scene from *The Lion King.*

We made it! We are in Orlando. The humidity. The freezing air conditioning. The Disney! We had poor luck with Magical Express during our 2005 trip and decided to use Happy Limousine again like we did when we came with Oliver in 2013. The great part is they do a stop at a grocery store or Walgreens so you can stock up on snacks, breakfast food, water, sodas, and all the toiletries you couldn't fit in your quart-size bag. Depending on your needs, you can also grab a few bottles of Prosecco and maybe a few beers. Then it's the ride into Walt Disney World.

Seeing those gates for the first time made us all bouncy and happy. That first Mickey sighting, watching Disney buses go by, and getting little peeks of the parks—the van could have been fueled by our excitement alone!

My mom and dad were staying at Coronado Springs, where they stayed during our last trip. They are big fans of the grounds that are filled with flowers, picturesque walkways, and a tasty, generous breakfast buffet. They talked about the beautiful walk to their room where they passed fountains and brightly colored flowers. It's also not very busy when there are not huge conventions, and this was one of those times. Something we love at every Disney resort is you are transported to a different world. Coronado Springs is teal, pink, and orange, and landscaped with famous Disney figures carved into the shrubbery. Our hotel was a much different world.

Driving toward Animal Kingdom Lodge, the landscape becomes more "African," with thick foliage and natural colors of brown, orange, and green. The entrance to Kidani Village looks like you are at a 4-star hotel on an African safari. The greeters are friendly and most have lilting accents. The resort even has an exotic smell, and the soundtrack is drumbeats with the occasional animal noise from the savannah.

We were nine hungry, tired, but super-excited people with a check-in time at least 4 or 5 hours away. So what do you do? You eat! And the eating at Kidani is delicious. This was my second time at Sanaa and I remembered how delicious it was.

For the grown-ups, our lunch at Sanaa started with cocktails. I had a Moscow Mule, served in the traditional copper mug, and it was exactly what I needed to get my shoulders to loosen up a bit. A Moscow Mule includes ginger beer, a hint of lime, and vodka. The ginger beer gives it some fizz and the sweet but tart lime with the small bit of heat from the ginger makes this the perfect refreshment on a warm day. We have multiple Shirley Temple drinkers in our group, but our waiter gave Nick and Austin a more grown-up way to order them: ask for a Grenadine with Sprite. On our second visit to Sanaa we had a great laugh when Nick ordered a Shirley Temple, Annie a kiddie cocktail, and Austin said in a very suave way, "A Grenadine and Sprite, please."

Our group loves bread, so we started with the full Indian-style bread service that offers a number of different breads including traditional naan, spiced naan, and paneer paratha. Naan is an Indian-style bread made by placing the dough on the insides of an incredibly hot tandoor, a clay oven that typically sits on the ground. The tandoor is incredibly hot and the bread dough is stuck to the oven walls. Naan is perfectly browned on the outside and a little crispy, while the inside is soft with big pockets of air perfect for scooping up delicious sauces. Naan is typically brushed with a bit of oil or butter.

The bread service comes with a wide selection of flavorful hummus, chutneys, jams, and dips. Our favorites were the mango and coriander chutneys. The mango chutney has a bite to it and the coriander chutney has a brightness that matched well with the paneer paratha.

Like most Disney restaurants, Sanaa is accommodating to dietary needs, whether it was Maggie's gluten free preference or Joe and I sharing because we had eaten too much of the bread service. We enjoyed the butter chicken and spiced lamb that the server had split into separate plates as we had a sleepy Oliver sitting between us. The butter chicken has chunks of juicy chicken that absorb the sauce, which is a mix of garam masala, stewed tomatoes, and cream.

During the meal we talked about the parks. Despite being so tired that we could all fall over, the decision was made to grab our bags, freshen up, and head to Magic Kingdom. The locker rooms at the pool had plenty of space for all of us to change and come out ready for the parks.

The Disney buses stop at Kidani Village first before going to the bigger and busier Animal Kingdom Lodge. At some resorts, the buses make multiple stops and so end up being very crowded, sometimes even too full for additional passengers. But Kidani Village was first on the resort's pick-up route, and some buses both pick up and drop off only at Kidani. Joe, the kids, and I were officially on our way. Nearing the Magic Kingdom, we caught glimpses of Animal Kingdom and Hollywood Studios and then we saw it, the gates to the Magic Kingdom.

Before our trip we received our MagicBands and everyone already had them on. Quite a few had put them on before brushing their teeth that morning. As we approached the Magic Kingdom, there was excited chatter about how the MagicBands work and all the cool things that can be done with them. We'd been together in September for my birthday, and everyone crowded around the computer and picked their MagicBand, a big debate erupting over who would get which color. The bands even have everyone's names printed inside them. Everyone felt how magical those bands were when we got to the gates, connected them to our fingerprints, and were in. Our group of nine stopped on Main Street to take it all in, get a few group photos in front of the castle, and a reaction video of everyone's face of that moment when you're walking down Main Street, feeling like you are entering a whole new world.

Every Disney trip has a few low points often involving people who have overdone it, exhausting themselves and their kids, and are just done but refuse to go home because they are going to get their money's worth, darn it! On our first day we ran into that family. We had a lot of fun enjoying Main Street, but then realized that a parade was about to start and that we needed to hurriedly get off the street. With cast members asking us to move and a wall of people and strollers giving us a dirty look as if challenging us to make our way past them, we just went for it and had a family angry with us. I apologized and told them we just wanted to get through and out of the way, not take their coveted spot.

While my parents were taking a little nap, the rest of us decided to head to Haunted Mansion for a little scare. Joe, Oliver, and I had a lot of fun in the line on our last trip and knew our big group would like it, too. The fun started with the busts of all the different characters and then continued with the instruments section. Annie especially liked playing with the books in the library.

After squeezing into our Doom Buggies, everyone enjoyed the spooks and ghouls of the Haunted Mansion. The ballroom scene with the ghosts dancing and dining is always my favorite.

After we exited, Nick said, "I've never been on Small World." That meant it was time to go on it. My parents had joined us by this time and were ready to face the Small World music. Now we *think* Nick was aware that Small World is not a thrill ride. However, after strategically placing him in the front row, the way he was death gripping the front bars one would think we were going to be taking on the hills of Splash Mountain. Not only did Nick get to experience Small World, we had a delay and had to sit in the last room for 5 minutes hearing that song. By the end of the ride, Nick was being serenaded by our entire group of 11 singing along.

Next was our FastPass+ for Big Thunder Mountain Railroad. I had read that with the addition of FP+, Big Thunder now has longer wait times. With the standby at over 50 minutes we were able to almost walk right on with our FastPass, which was good because the 3 a.m. start was starting to take its toll on the group. This was one of the few rides I actually got to sit with Austin and the two of us had a great time screaming our heads off. The new version seems faster and longer, with more drops and tighter turns. We all came off happy, but it wasn't the kids who were excited for the next ride, it was my parents. Their nap came in handy and while they stayed at the park to use our FP+ for Seven Dwarfs Mine Train and Wishes (the nighttime fireworks show), our group of nine headed back to our hotel.

Prior to choosing Kidani Village I heard about the long walks to the room. By this time everyone was tired and ready to unpack, eat, and veg. Well, it was not to be. The group headed to the elevator knowing that our room was at the end, but having no idea what we were in for.

The nine of us emerged from the elevator like a carful of clowns and start-ing walking the halls, checking out the decorations folks had put on their doors, looking at the animals, anticipation building with each step. Austin, Oliver, and Nate ran ahead. And we walked. And walked. And walked. It just kept going and going. We were in the last room to the left of the lobby. Literally, the last room. You could go no further than our room. You would be outside with the wildebeests if you went past our room. After using the pedometer for the next hike, we found out it was 1/3 of a mile from our room to the elevators. Not from the buses or the lobby, from the elevators.

By this time the boys were already in the room. "I opened the door with my band!" exclaimed Oliver the second that Joe, the girls, and I walked in. The room was beautiful and shockingly had enough space for all nine of us. The cast member at check-in was able to get us the true two-bedroom villa, instead of a one-bedroom with a studio lock-off. There was a lot of dark wood, burnt oranges, and dark reds with crisp white linens. The bed in the master was tall and plush with a ton of pillows. The mural of an African savannah at sunset on the tile in the bathroom was a stunning array of bright orange and yellow with hints of red and the dark brown outlines of tress.

Oliver said something he wanted to remember from today was "when we saw our hotel room and the bathroom in my parent's room." The fact that the master had a separate room for the toilet came in handy when nine people are trying to get ready in the morning. There was ample closet space in the bathroom and a large dresser that fit my clothes as well as Joe and Oliver's. The second bedroom had two queen-size beds and two closets, with the sink separate from the bath/shower and toilet. Again, very handy. There was also a full bath right near the front door that Austin and Maggie used. Austin commandeered the pull-out chair in the living room and Maggie took the pull-out couch. We used the kitchen for quick breakfasts and snacks.

> **TIP!** If you're booking a Disney Vacation Club Villa, check out one of the websites with the floor plans prior to departing, especially if you're with a large group. Some of the rooms at Kidani, for example, didn't have two queens in the second bedroom because they weren't a true two-bedroom; they were a one-bedroom with a studio lock-off. It's worth doing the extra research and making the request to reservations *before* your trip. They may not be able to accommodate every request, but if you have the max number of folks for a room, they will typically try and prioritize you.

But the part that was unlike any other hotel room in the world, except maybe Africa, was the long balcony that looked out onto the savannah. And not just any part of the savannah, the very end where all the animals are kept when not out roaming. That day we saw a pack of gazelles bounding across the savannah to get their evening meal and two giraffes with their necks intertwined standing under a tree. The baby warthog and his family were just to the left of our balcony and though noisy, were adorable. That night the baby was expressing its extreme displeasure at being in the cage by squealing loudly for about 30 minutes. It was so cute we didn't even mind. At one point there was a parade of giraffes, zebras, gazelles, and wildebeests with a few ostriches all meandering to their cages, about

15 yards from where the nine of us were standing. "Zebras!" "Giraffes!" "Look at the giraffes eating out of the tree! Their tongues are so long". It was a chorus of voices as all 9 of us stood on the balcony in disbelief as the sun set and the animals were making their trek home. This is what Disney does; it transports you to another world.

Dinner that night was room service. Another highlight of each Disney resort is that the room service is a little different and themed to the resort. As *Monsters University* played in the background (I don't think we left the Disney channel the whole trip), Nate, Austin, and Nick chowed down on burgers, naan, and my favorite, tandoori nachos. The sauce that comes with the bread is perfect for opening up the nasal passages. It has a kick, but at the end of a day of travel was exactly what congested Sam needed. Before bed, we told everyone that Epcot was on the agenda for tomorrow and we needed to be out of the hotel at 8:30 for our 9:15 a.m. Mission:SPACE FastPass. Then Oliver climbed into bed with us (the older kids were still too excited to sleep) and we passed out.

CHAPTER EIGHTEEN
Eating Our Way Through Epcot

Day 2

Sam, Nate, Maggie, and I were quite excited for today because Epcot is Nate and Maggie's favorite park and Sam and I were salivating for the Food & Wine Festival. The Food & Wine propaganda started right at the entrance to Epcot. There was a huge display of posters from each country in the Food & Wine Festival in the space near the Leave a Legacy area. But before we could stuff our faces it was time for a space showdown at Mission: SPACE.

Oliver is our space fanatic and has been able to name the planets in order since he was two. This was the first ride that he had been to small to board when we came in 2013. "The best part of today was Mission: SPACE because it was really cool and awesome and really fun. We actually went into space," exclaimed Oliver after Mission: SPACE, which he viewed as an older kid ride. Joe, Nick, Annie, and I were in one group, while Nate, Sam, Austin and Oliver were in their own pod. Somehow, this became a competition with everyone talking smack and pretending to throw down in the hallway before heading into our pod.

I find Mission: SPACE interesting and have always liked the feeling of the G-forces, but as I get older, I find it makes me a bit claustrophobic. I'm not a fan of the pressure it places on my chest. My dad has gotten to a point where he doesn't do many of the thrill rides and though Mom did this one with us in 2005, they both decided to skip Mission: SPACE for a bit of extra time to linger outside and enjoy breakfast at their hotel.

Mission: SPACE exits into a space-themed area with video games and a playground. For one of the games you split into two teams of four and compete on fixing a spaceship by moving colored circles around on a huge screen. Nate, Sam, Oliver, and Nick were on one team; Austin, Joe, Maggie, and Annie were on another. Annie and Austin are gamers, but it's definitely not Joe and Maggie's thing. The other team was a group of huge video game fans. Austin is super-competitive so was excited when their team won. Joe was even more thrilled because "the old man beat a group of video game addicts!" This is one of the many reasons for you to make time to just walk around and linger because some of the most magical moments occur when you least expect it.

Like many attractions, Mission: SPACE exits into a store, a treasure trove of space fun and even a few *Star Wars* pieces. Epcot has so much to get through on a regular trip, but add in all the tastes to experience with Food & Wine and it's difficult to do everything in one day. In addition to Soarin', Spaceship Earth and the clay warriors in China, Epcot has incredible shopping. From toys in Japan, to space shirts by Mission: SPACE, to a store devoted to Frozen in Norway, you can spend a lot of time shopping.

> **TIP!** A great place to go to the bathroom in the morning is the Electric Umbrella restaurant. Before it's open it's quiet, very clean, and in a great central location when you're in Future World.

After Mission:SPACE, we reunited with my parents and the 11 of us hurried over to the Food & Wine Festival pavilion. If you are at the park early before World Showcase opens at 11 a.m., and in dire need of a Food & Wine Festival fix because you have been so excited for this portion of the trip, the pavilion can sate you. For a time. The pavilion is home to all things Food & Wine. There is a stand to pick up your Food & Wine passports, as well as books with all the events and offerings at the Food & Wine marketplaces. The passport is a lot of fun and a great souvenir of your Food & Wine experience. At each marketplace you can get stamps and there is a list in the passport so you can check off all the tasty things you have tried and have a memento of your gluttony. (I love checking things off a list!)

The pavilion is also home to the Ghirardelli space with its chocolate sculptures and free chocolate. The chocolate sculptures are amazing. They are different every year and always timely to the latest that Disney has to offer. There are a number of *Up* fanatics in our group, so Carl's house with the balloons and colors we had never seen in chocolate drew gasps. Along with the sculptures and friendly cast members with baskets of samples, you can also try drinking chocolate. As our sweet tooth champ, Austin was keen to try the drinking chocolate and excitedly purchased a few cups for the group to try. "That is not what I was expecting," said a disappointed Austin as he realized drinking chocolate does NOT taste like a melted Hershey bar." The dark chocolate fans in the group took a few sips, but Grandma and Joe, being the good sports, finished the cups so Austin would feel that the purchase was worthwhile.

There are a lot of ways to part with your money at the pavilion and one fun way was buying Sam the Remy's Ratatouille Hide & Squeak game board. This is one of the ways Disney is trying to make Food & Wine more kid friendly. There are Remys hidden at many of the marketplaces and using the provided food-themed stickers, you track where you have found him.

Once Sam had found all of the Remys, she would get a prize. This became one more thing we loved doing at Food & Wine. Some Remys were quite easy and others required a little assistance from fellow guests. If you're looking for a way to make some new Food & Wine Festival friends, this is a good one. Between cast members who didn't even know who Remy is and walked out of their kiosks to help us search, to guests young and old giving each other tips, Remy is a master at bringing folks together.

It was time for most of the kids to experience The Seas with Nemo & Friends ride for the first time. The song "Big Blue World" became a hit, especially for Maggie. Our next stop was Soarin', where Austin learned the hard way to listen closely to directions as he spent the ride wearing the safety strap. The safety strap is designed to keep little kids, those well under five feet tall, safe. At almost 5'9," Austin did not enjoy the ride as much as he normally would and was walking funny for a bit afterwards.

> **TIP!** Try and sit in the very front row of Soarin' if possible. This is the row that goes the highest. It also helps avoid experiencing the attraction with feet dangling in your face if you happen to be sitting under a very tall guest.

After Soarin', our quick-donut-in-the-room breakfast was wearing off—it was time for food. Food and Wine was in full swing and we were ready to hit the marketplaces. There are 25 of them spread throughout World Showcase and a few other locations in Epcot. These small kiosks serve tasty treats from all over the world. Each marketplace typically has 3–5 dishes, at least one being dessert, and different cocktails and wines. World Showcase and Food & Wine is not really Austin's thing and my folks thought the Food & Wine Festival sounded cool but weren't hugely interested, so we split up. Austin, Mom, and Dad headed to lunch at the Coral Reef Restaurant. "I felt bad enjoying this delectable salmon while watching fish swim by," Dad said, even though it did not change how delicious he thought it was. By this point Austin was itching to get out of Epcot and after a few great pictures, including one from across the lagoon that makes it look like Austin is holding up Spaceship Earth, they headed over to Disney Springs.

Disney Springs was a huge hit for the group. They saw a variety of performers and did a lot of shopping and eating. It's always a bit surprising that Austin really enjoys shopping on vacation and he always buys souvenirs for family and friends. The only time he spends money on himself is to buy something involving sugar. During their Disney Springs trek, my folks and Austin visited the Christmas shop, the Wonderful World of Disney, and the Ghirardelli chocolate shop.

Back at Epcot, Sam and I had our Food & Wine passports and were determined to get as many stamps and check off as many dishes as possible.

Having come from the bold flavors of Sanaa and the room service at our hotel, our palates were awake and ready for bold flavors. Disney food has to appeal to a wide variety, so it's a toss up of whether a restaurant is going to be authentic or have mass crowd appeal. Our expectation was Food and Wine Festival wouldn't hold back and we would experience tasty Disney magic.

The first taste started at Sustainable Chew. This marketplace features what Joe calls chef food or tweezer food because it involves ingredients that can be tricky to find in most grocery stores and the plating requires the steady hand of a brain surgeon with an art degree. So our first dish of many that day was pork sparerib with red wine, fennel, and cheesy mascarpone grits. The spareribs were fall off the bone tender and the grits were smooth and creamy, but overall it could have used a bit more flavor. The vanilla panna cotta with fresh figs and pistachio brittle was a sweet contrast to the salty sparerib. The panna cotta was super creamy and the pistachio brittle gave a nice salty crunch. It was all delicious but was large and a bit difficult to eat while the plate was balanced on my knees.

Then it was onto Ireland. The food at the Ireland marketplace was not the fancy stuff Irish gastropubs are serving now, but the stick-to-your-ribs classic lobster and seafood fisherman's pie that had mashed potatoes with the broiled top like a shepard's pie. It may not have been my favorite of the day, but I was so hungry I could hear my stomach growling, so Joe, Oliver, and I devoured the Irish cheese selection plate and the warm chocolate pudding within seconds.

Remembering our delicious dinner with unique flavors at Restaurant Marrakesh in 2005, I was ready for Morocco to surprise and delight. The harissa chicken roll is the Moroccan version of an egg roll and it did not disappoint. The outside was a crispy pastry with a moist chicken, corn, cilantro, harissa, and cheese on the inside. I love roasted red peppers, and this is a dominant flavor in harissa. I paired this with a mimosa royale featuring champagne and orange juice.

The next stop was Brazil and the escondidinho de carne "little hidden one" layered meat pie with mashed yucca. Brazilian food is typically delicious, but this meat pie was in a bowl with decently flavored ground beef, similar to a homemade taco, and a sad dollop of hardened mashed potatoes. On the flip side, the frozen caipirinha was great. It featured cachaça, the famous Brazilian pure sugar cane spirit that makes mixed drinks quite dangerous. Brazil is one of the countries I would love to see added to the World Showcase to provide much-needed representation for South America. There could be a steakhouse to give Le Cellier a run for its money, stores with great fashion, and the dangerously delicious caipirinha.

Now it was onto Mexico and the tacos de camaron featuring lightly fried shrimp, pico de gallo, pickled onions and chipotle mayo in a flour tortilla. The taco was delicious, one of the best bites of the day; although $5.50 seemed a bit steep for a tiny taco, it packed a flavorful punch and was Joe's favorite taste of the day. The shrimp was sweet, the mayo had the right amount of spice, and there was a nice crunch from the piquant onions. Each bite was a mix of creamy, crunchy, and sweet with a hint of salt from the shrimp batter and the tortilla.

One of the challenges of Food & Wine is the lack of seating. Now a cheese plate from Ireland or a taco from Mexico are on-the-go friendly, but trying to eat short ribs with a knife and fork balanced on your kid's head takes away from the experience a bit. We did find a few hidden seating gems that can make your tasting experience more enjoyable. Joe, Oliver, and I enjoyed tacos on the steps of Mexico's pyramid; pastries on the ledge around the fountain in France, which has the added benefit of typically being a bit cooler because of the water; the benches by the warrior museum in China, with their shade and scenic view; and the crates outside of the African outpost, a welcome respite when you're in the long stretch between countries. Or you can just stand in a circle taking bites.

Annie and Nick hit the Japan Marketplace numerous times and the sushi, especially the tempura shrimp roll, were their favorites. The roll was inside out with cucumber and tempura-fried shrimp finished with teriyaki sauce. They also sampled the spicy hand roll with tuna and salmon and kazan volcano sauce.

Budget-conscious stepmother moment here. I knew this was going to be a pricey food day as everyone was split up with their MagicBands trying a lot of new foods and racking up charges. There were a few times Joe had to tell me to stop worrying and just enjoy. A lot of folks suggest buying a gift card and managing the spending that way. We decided to just channel Elsa's "let it go" and deal with the consequences on next month's Disney Visa bill. Honestly, it didn't end up being as expensive as I had thought it would be. One tip is to watch the amount spent on bottled drinks. Disney must make a killing on those. Having everyone start the day with a drink from the room can cut about $3 per person from the daily tab. Super-responsible folks will hang onto that bottle and refill it at a much lower cost.

Maggie is the one in our group who went "down under" to the Australia marketplace. With her gluten sensitivity, she is our resident restricted diet expert and was impressed by the multitude of offerings at Disney. Every sit-down restaurant offered a gluten-free menu and the vast offerings of tasty treats at the Food and Wine Festival marketplaces was the most variety Maggie's taste buds had experienced in a while. The shrimp in Australia had been on my list, but my feet, the heat, and the building crowds were getting to us. Then, Maggie appeared with the grilled sweet-and-spicy bush berry shrimp with pineapple, pepper, onion, and snap peas, and

I was able to steal a bite. The shrimp was perfectly grilled, the toppings offered an interesting mix of flavors, and the sauce added a nice zing. To me, it was not as good as the shrimp taco, but did receive our gluten-free expert's stamp of approval.

South Korea, our last marketplace, wins the award for the best bite. Joe, Annie, Nick, Nate, Sam, Oliver, and I liked every offering, and it was home to my favorite taste of the day. Prior to the trip I had done my research and read up on every food marketplace. I had a list of all the things I wanted to try. As with most things Disney, the list was a bit aggressive and we would have spent the entire day standing in marketplace lines.

So, South Korea was on the long list, but not an A priority. Was I wrong. We ended up sending Annie and Nick back in line for seconds and then thirds. Joe, Oliver, Nate, Sam, Annie, Nick, and I stood in a circle sharing the roasted pork lettuce wrap and kimchi slaw. The flavors packed a punch and the mix of the juicy Korean-spiced pork with crunchy vegetables and a creamy sauce took my taste buds on a roller coaster. The wrap was refreshing, tasty, and healthy. We also sampled the bulgogi BBQ short rib with steamed rice and cucumber kimchi. The kimchi added a nice freshness, crunch, and contrast to the heaviness of the BBQ sauce on the meat. Our last taste was the soju banana milkshake with ginger soother that Oliver enjoyed a few sips of until we started asking each other, "Is there alcohol in that?" Whoops. Joe and Nate finished it.

I would have liked to try every single one of the dishes and cocktails on offer at Food & Wine. There were over 30 different cocktails, and even more wines, beers, and liquors like sake and vodka. Prior to the trip, I had made a list of what I wanted to try and it was so long I had to prioritize. On my list were 31 dishes or cocktails our group needed to try. We spent from 9:15 a.m. to almost 7 p.m. at Epcot, primarily in World Showcase, and I tried 12 of them.

The biggest misses were the empanada in Patagonia; the Berbere-style beef tenderloin and buttered chicken with naan in Africa; lechon asado, the soufflé, and the frozen sugar cane cocktail in the Dominican Republic; the strawberry-basil champagne toast in Desserts & Champagne; the créme brulée and ice pop pomme in France; the lamb meatball in New Zealand; the haggis in Scotland; the liquid nitro chocolate-almond truffle in the Chew Lab, and the frozen caipirinha in Brazil. Food & Wine really is a multiple day excursion, especially if you have more than 10 items on your list of new tastes to experience.

Also, go once the sun has gone down and it's cooler. Joe and I love food. We travel for food. We planned our last three vacations to include cities known for great food. There was so much to be excited about during the trip that I didn't realize until I was home how many more dishes I wish I had been able to try. And when it's hot you just eat less. Though all the food was tasty, cheddar soup in 90-degree heat is not a winner. Had our feet not been ready to fall off and the 1/3 mile walk back to the room looming ahead, I may have been able to make another trip around the Showcase when it was cooler, and a lamb meatball with spicy tomato chutney would have hit the spot!

I also missed having a sit-down meal together this day. There is a new small plates restaurant in Morocco that would have been fun, or even Restaurant Marrakech again (and seeing Austin's reaction to the belly dancer now). This was the only day on the whole trip that we didn't have at least one family meal, and looking back I think that is why it was one of my least favorite days of the trip. While planning, it was the day I was looking forward to the most, but not having that focused time together left a hole in the day.

Joe, Nate, Sam, Maggie, Annie, Nick, Oliver, and I wrapped our Food & Wine culinary adventure with one more taco from Mexico and then started the return trek to the room, debating whether to ride Spaceship Earth before we left. We stopped at a few stores on the way out and got Oliver a Perry from *Phineas & Ferb* that makes his signature chattering sound, Annie a black hoodie with the signature structures from each park in silver and white, and a few small gifts for friends back home.

Despite having clocked 11 miles already that day (Annie was keeping track on her phone pedometer), the group decided to give our feet a break on Spaceship Earth. All of us had seen Illuminations, some of us multiple times, but today no one was up for staying and battling even worse crowds. We got a few great pictures in front of the Epcot sphere, which was glowing in pinks and purples against the night sky, compared photos of the day on the bus, and dragged ourselves across the animal-print carpets of Kidani Village to our room. As Oliver said, "This vacation is off to a really great start!"

CHAPTER NINETEEN
Shopping and Singing in the Studios

Day 3

Mom, the thrill-seeker grandma, was the most excited for today because we were riding her favorite Disney ride, Tower of Terror, first. This was Sam's first time on the ride and she was terrified—so terrified that she gripped the hand bars through the beginning film about the story of the hotel and haunted elevator, through the short ride into the twilight zone, and gripped even tighter as our car rose up and then fell multiple stories, then rose and fell again, our whole car screaming as the doors opened and the sun and warmth streamed in. She was still gripping the hand bars, breathless and shaking, as we made our short trip out of the twilight zone and to the unloading area. Even after the ride was completely stopped and the doors were opened, she was still gripping the hand bars.

The next ride was much more enjoyable for Sam. The whole family was eagerly awaiting Star Tours because there are a number of *Star Wars* fans in the group. The waiting area for Star Tours is a mix of indoor and outdoor spaces. The outdoor space transports you into the Ewok village with high trees and rocks that can be a great place to rest your feet. Once inside, it's a different world. After your eyes adapt from the sun, you will see that you are in a busy spaceport offering space vacations or "star tours." There are posters for different destinations, luggage, and a replica star cruiser with an R2 unit. As you wind around the spaceport you're brought to a long hallway that serves as the star cruiser loading area. A cast member hands you 3D glasses and advises you not to put them on until you're seated on the ride. That is a running theme here. From the time you get the glasses to the start of the ride, you may hear that warning about five times. (And after watching someone from another group almost trip and face plant into a seat during boarding, I understand why.)

Before the ride gets moving, the mission is announced. One of your fellow riders is identified as a rebel fugitive. You know who it is because they shine a beam of light directly on this person and their photo shows up on the screens at the front of the cruiser. Sam was our rebel! This was Sam's first time on the ride and so it took her a moment and Nate poking her before she even knew she was a wanted woman.

Finally, the ride begins and you spend the next few minutes being rocketed and tossed around as you are taken to recognizable lands from *Star Wars*. You successfully escape Darth Vader's powers and are thrown back against your seat as the cruiser hits hyper speed. At the end of the lighted tunnel you enter a new world. As Oliver wrote in his journal, "On Star Wars we went to Hoth and then I went again with Nick and we went to the Clone Wars battle." Suddenly the empire's forces attack and your cruiser turns left and right sharply to avoid AT-ATs and over-zealous Stormtroopers. After a visit to another land you safely arrive at the rebel base and are once again reminded to take off your glasses before attempting to depart the cruiser.

The ride exits into a store (of course) called Tatooine Traders that is a haven for any *Star Wars* fan. Be prepared to hang out in this store for a while. Our average time in Tatooine Traders is at least an hour. You can build your own droid with fun parts like Yoda Mickey ears, build your own lightsaber, and find the Star Wars Disney set with Leia Minnie, Vader Goofy, and Luke Mickey.

After the first of a few shopping trips at Tatooine Traders, we decided that 10:30 a.m. was the perfect time for an ice cream. There is a cart near the entrance to the Indiana Jones Epic Stunt Spectacular that has all the park favorites: Mickey ear-shaped vanilla ice cream with a crunchy semisweet chocolate coating, Mickey-shaped ice cream sandwiches, and even frozen bananas covered in chocolate.

Since everyone in our group is a *Frozen* fanatic, the next stop was the Frozen Sing-Along. And it was a sing-a-long, a words-on-the-screen, actors-on-stage-singing, kids-in-the-front-row-out-of-their-seats-dancing sing-a-long. Except we seemed to be in the one show with a crowd that either didn't understand or didn't appreciate sing-a-longs. October is a big month for travelers from Latin America and perhaps the preference was to hear the actors instead of Maggie and Joe belting out each song.

The end of the show is enchanting. While it snows in the theatre, all of the actors, including Queen Elsa, are on stage singing "Let It Go." With the snowflakes projections on the walls, epic music, soft blue lighting, and snow falling from the sky, you feel as if you are with Elsa on the mountaintop about to build your own ice castle. We had this little boy in front of us that stood up with his hands raised above his head when Elsa is doing her big finale. It was perfect.

Our next stop was Pixar Place and Toy Story Mania. Now I have mixed feelings about this ride. I love the line. It makes you feel like you've been shrunk down and are playing in one of the most iconic Disney/Pixar movie sets, Andy's room. The loading area is multi-story fun, but I wish you could have a bit more time in there for pictures. Toy Story Mania is akin to sitting in a racing carnival ride while trying to play carnival games at the same time. Like PhilharMagic and It's Tough to Be a Bug, the ride is 4D so you don 3D glasses, smell freshly baked pie in the air, have rockets shot at you, and feel gusts of air when guns fire and even a few droplets of water in the water gun game. Unlike the Buzz Lightyear ride in Magic Kingdom, which many guests complain is too difficult, the firing mechanism here involves pulling a ball at the end of the string to fire. Though easier than Buzz, it can be tricky to aim as the guns are pretty high and younger kids may be frustrated with low scores.

This is one of the most popular attractions in all of Disney World and definitely worth using a FastPass, though we had to wait for about 20 minutes in the FastPass line. It's not worth waiting the upwards of 70 minutes you can often expect in the stand-by line, unless you really love *Toy Story*.

Lunch was at Nate's favorite restaurant, Sci-Fi Dine-In Theatre. On our trip in 2005, we had no problems being able to get our group of nine all together in the 1950's-inspired car tables. Always make sure to ask to sit in a car when you make the reservation and when you check in. Sitting in the cars while watching the old movies really makes the experience. The cars only seat nine and despite requesting to sit together and waiting an extra 20 minutes, we were put in cars away from each other. Sadly, a lot of the hostesses aren't familiar with the set-up in the dining room so don't understand how the numbering works.

Not being together, especially when the car next to ours was open, put me in a bad mood, so the habanero lime margarita was just what the Disney doctor ordered. The drink was crisp and refreshing, with saltiness from the margarita mix. The subtle heat from the habanero kept it from getting too sweet. Sci-Fi is definitely a burger joint and the servings are generous. Unless you're starving, you can probably get away with sharing. There are a lot of other options on the menu like a New York strip steak, pastas, and a salmon BLT. The onion rings are a must. They are always straight from the fryer so the outside is crisp, the onions are sweet, and they pair well with a quick dip in a pool of ketchup.

After lunch, we decided to split up for a bit. Joe, Oliver, and I went to the Phineas & Ferb meet and greet. Standing in line for characters isn't a big thing with our group. We get excited when we see them walking around the park (and of course we have Annie with her Tigger obsession), but, in general, we don't spend too much time waiting in line for autographs.

Phineas & Ferb are a blast. Their character space looks like a TV set that resembles their backyard, with a huge tree, bright green grass, and a yellow fence over which an animatronic Perry the Platypus will peek every few minutes. If you haven't watched Phineas & Ferb, you really should. It's fun for all ages. It's witty and there is a lot of interesting variety with the characters from Ferb the young British brother who says about 10 words per episode to the obnoxious older sister Candace to the young Indian genius with a high voice, Baljeet. Phineas and Ferb are boy-genius brothers with a knack for inventions like a Styrofoam skate park, a time machine, or a roller coaster that was stuck together with peanut butter.

But the best part is the music. Hits like "104 Days of Summer," "S.I.M.P., or Squirrels in My Pants," "There's a Platypus Controlling Me," or the song playing while Phineas & Ferb ride through Candace's body in a tiny submarine that features the lyric, "Don't want to make a fuss but that was the pancreas, slow down before we reach the colon." The meet and greet is an homage to the witty, inventive music on the show, with the brothers' playful personalities on display as music blares. They often pause from signing autographs to break out into dance. Phineas & Ferb had a great time with Oliver because he didn't walk or run to them, he danced over to them, and then spent half of his time showing them his moves. The wrangler actually had to stop the three of them to have Phineas & Ferb sign an autograph.

Austin, Annie, Nick, and I tried Rock 'n' Roller Coaster which was having issues most of our trip. This was the first of two attempts for this ride. The four of us stood in line for about 45 minutes, during which we moved about 25 steps. We gave up and decided it was time for a bit of movie magic and so we met up with the rest of the group to go on the Great Movie Ride.

When I was a kid I loved the Great Movie Ride. Seeing all the different movies, the live-action gunfight, and that alien scared me every time. You enter through a replica of Grauman's Chinese Theatre and board a tram in front of a larger-than-life 1930's neon theatre marquee. The tram transports you into scenes from some of the most famous movies in history. Along for the ride is a tour guide who offers humorous commentary and fills in the spaces between the pre-recorded narration. Ours was a typical not-very-exciting ride through the movies with a female guide who was delivering an okay show. And then we entered the gangster scene, resembling the backstreets of 1930's Chicago. Here we met our Muggsy, the most flamboyant gangster any of us had ever experienced. He was a serious source of amusement for Joe and Nate as the gangster character is written to be a very tough, gun-slinging criminal. In the scene where the gangster goes to retrieve the large jewel in the Raiders of the Lost Ark scene, we saw the full extent of this young man's dance training as he struck a pose with the flair and exuberance of Liza in *Cabaret*.

Now it was time for shopping. Hollywood Boulevard features a row of great shops and is close to another row of shops on Sunset Boulevard.

Like Main Street at Magic Kingdom, these boulevards transport you to another time and place with an Old Hollywood vibe. My favorite shop is Keystone Clothiers on Hollywood Boulevard. It offers a variety of clothing not found in many other shops, and was one of the few places we could find a Disney shirt that fit Joe's style.

Joe isn't throwing on the sneakers and fanny pack anytime soon, so for him to wear anything souvenir-like is pretty rare. At Keystone I found a great button-down shirt for him that was off-white with black hand-drawn symbols for each park and some of the lands and attractions within them. It's the perfect shirt for the person who will not wear Mickey ears or a Goofy t-shirt, but who still wants to bring a little magic into the office with them.

Now it was time for Fantasmic! We arrived more than 30 minutes before the show started, but the seats in the front section were already full. After scoping out our options, most which were at the very far end of the theatre, we chose to sit at the back of the stadium in the middle. Though the view of the canoes on the lake was a bit limited, everyone was able to stand on the benches and had plenty of room for dancing during the show.

Annie and I were in charge of snacks and she finally got her Mickey pretzel. It's a bit disconcerting how many times a day we are gnawing on something shaped like our favorite mouse's head, but his ears dipped in a bit of cheese sauce was the perfect showtime snack. Annie especially enjoyed the show, because she didn't remember it from our 2005 trip. It was like her first time all over again. A favorite moment for the group was when a black-and-white boat with Mickey dressed as Steamboat Willie emerges. Though it feels very 1920s, it is filled with princesses in their colorful, glittery gowns, handsome princes in their finery, and characters happily waving and dancing.

TIP! Use the end of Fantasmic! as a time to take a seat. It takes awhile for that stadium to empty out and your choice is to stand in a slow-moving line for over 20 minutes on sore feet or sit and take a breath. I recommend you sit for at least 10 minutes. Finish up your popcorn and drinks and have a chat about the highlights of the show. Once the people at the far end of the stadium are finally making their way out, or cast members are sweeping around you, then it's time to leave. This can even help relieve some of the bus congestion because everyone leaving Fantasmic! is typically heading right to the bus line. Your feet will thank you.

CHAPTER TWENTY
The Best FastPass+ Decision Ever Made

Day 4

Everyone had different things they wanted to do during the day, so we split up. Joe and Oliver headed to Hollywood Studios for more Star Tours. Nate and Sam went to Epcot for more Food & Wine and for lunch at San Angel Inn in the Mexico pavilion. Sam was determined to find all those Remys and get her prize. Annie and Nick and Mom and Dad also headed back to Epcot. Mags took some time alone with the giraffes and did a little writing while Austin and I decided to give Rock 'n' Roller Coaster another try. Sadly, this resulted in a 30-minute wait, and just as we were rounding the corner to get into the loading area, the ride broke. Second day in a row. We decided to give up and headed to the Starbucks in Hollywood Studios to make ourselves feel better. After a coffee frap for me, a caramel frap for Austin, and bacon, egg, and goudas for us both, we did a bit of Austin's other favorite vacation activity: shopping.

This is when I spotted them, the shoe ornaments. On an earlier trip I purchased these fun pajama pants that feature a designer shoe for Ariel, Aurora, Belle, Cinderella, Jasmine, Rapunzel, Snow White, and Tinker Bell. The PJ pants are one of my favorite Disney souvenirs, so when I spotted a full display of at least 20 different shoes in ornament form at the Celebrity 5 & 10 Shop, my day was made and my camera was full. I took an embarrassing amount of photos of those shoes, like first-time-seeing-Cinderella-Castle number of photos. The actual designs are a bit different from the PJ pants, but the style is similar, very intricate with a lot of detailing that captures the style of the character.

Each shoe is unique and a fun way to enjoy the detail and thought animators put into having the fashion of the character match their personality. Even the villains have shoes. I love a great princess gown, but the shoes for the villains reflected the designers having a great time. Jack Skellington's is black and white and the toes look like a fancy tux with a thin bowtie and a heel of bones, and Malificent's has a purple base and black lace toe with lime green details. Whether it's princesses or evil queens, you can part with a lot of your vacation budget collecting these little beauties.

Surprisingly, Austin did not share in my enjoyment and appreciation of Disney fashion, so we bought him a football he had been eyeing and decided to explore some of the nearby hotels. We hopped on a boat and headed over to the Boardwalk Inn. Straight back from the pier is a large green lawn in front of the main building of the inn. Austin and I played catch on the lawn near the boat dock and talked about the trip. This was one of those memorable moments where you just stop and enjoy the people you are with. Yes, there are fireworks, plunging elevators, and castles, but some of the most magical moments are the simple ones, like playing catch with your teenager in the Florida sunshine. We walked around the BoardWalk and a few of the shops and then took the boat back to Hollywood Studios. First, though, we saw where Joe and I got married. I wish Joe and I had made time to head over there and steal a moment with each other, but it was nice to be able to see a peek of it.

As we waited in line at Hollywood Studios for the bus to our hotel, Austin started playing catch with three little kids. There were two little girls about 6 and 4 with a little boy who was maybe 3. Come to find out they were from Scotland. The four of them kept the game going the entire bus ride. At one point the mom told me, "You have a good one there." Before we got off the bus at Kidani Village, the little boy gave Austin a huge hug. How many places will a 15-year-old from a Chicago suburb get to play catch with three little kids from Scotland?

After walking almost a mile to get to the room and then back to the pool, Austin and I were seriously regretting we didn't pack swimsuits or wear them under our clothes. The pool at Kidani Village is huge. There is an entire water play area that has places to climb around. There are a few slides hidden away in the rocks that deposit you into a zero-entry pool. There is also a giant Jacuzzi that, according to Oliver, "could totally fit a bunch of hippos if they came over from the Animal Kingdom." Like most Disney pools, there is entertainment with prizes for the kids. Austin and I dominated the balloon toss and won a Disney prize. In between asking incessantly about going to Typhoon Lagoon or Disney Springs, Austin was quite the eye candy for a high school girl there with her family.

Austin and I grabbed a late lunch at the Maji Pool Bar of pulled pork sandwiches and chips. When you are starving and swimming everything tastes delicious, but that pulled pork was the perfect mix of tangy, sweet BBQ sauce with a bag of crunchy chips. Maggie and I indulged in a few signature Disney cocktails. I'm not a huge fan of super sweet cocktails, and the piña colada inspired drink was definitely on the sweet side but, when you're sitting in the sunshine at a pool that resembles a water hole in Africa, an icy tropical treat with hints of pineapple and coconut is apropos.

Slowly everyone started to trickle back to the hotel with tales of their day. Oliver and Joe rode Star Tours five times, purchased a few more Star Wars souvenirs, and lunched at Pizza Planet—a perfect day in Oliver's world. Nate found that "being in the Japan pavilion reminded me how much I love chubby Asian kids, like Russell in *Up!*" Sam found all of her Remys at Food & Wine and got her prize, a Remy pin. Annie and Nick did more shopping and Nick did get a chance to go on a few rides.

By this time the group was tired and a bit grumpy, but it was time to head to the Magic Kingdom and another go at Big Thunder Mountain, with a quick stop at Mickey's PhilharMagic first. Even the most tired and grumpy of the group couldn't resist enjoying swirling through their favorite Disney movies like *Little Mermaid*, *Aladdin*, and *Lion King*. Magic Kingdom was packed by this time because the Mickey's Not-So-Scary Halloween Party was happening quite a few evenings during this week, and today was one of the few days that you could be in the park for the projections and fireworks without paying the additional cost for the party, which for our big party would have been upwards of $500.

I hadn't made any dinner reservations, but had read good things about Columbia Harbour House, which was close by. The fried shrimp was crispy on the outside and sweet on the inside with a tangy cocktail sauce. Annie, Austin, and Nick all enjoyed the chicken pot pie, and though I don't like broccoli, even I thought my mom's crunchy broccoli salad was tasty and had the added benefit of getting a little green into my Disney diet. The kids found a cozy booth that we could all squeeze into. With a few chairs around the end of the table, everyone was able to hear each other and shared tales of their day.

> **TIP!** Try to eat meals at weird times. Unless you have reservations, having dinner before 6 or after 8:30 p.m., or lunch before 11 or after 2 p.m., can save you a lot of time in food lines. Almost every quick-service location has seating or there is seating nearby. So split up and have one group order while the other finds a place to sit. Once you are sitting down, stop and take a minute to enjoy each other's company. Have a chat about something new you have experienced, what pictures you're posting on Instagram, and what you want to make sure not to miss.

All of us left the restaurant in a much better mood and the excitement for Seven Dwarfs Mine Train and Celebrate the Magic was building. To waste a bit of time before our FP+, we headed over to the Enchanted Tiki Room. This is a great attraction in which to cool off, digest, and rest your feet before battling the parade and fireworks crowds. The Enchanted Tiki Room is one of those Disney classics that is always being messed with. The music feels very 70s, the room has a vintage smell, and it's so low-tech you can actually hear the clicking as the birds move. And I love it. Our whole group did. Neither Sam nor Nick had ever been regaled by the birds of the Enchanted Tiki Room and Sam once again had her Disney face on and Nick had his now famous Small World look of an open-mouth, wide eyes, and amazement.

It was time to make the trek into Fantasyland and my handy Disney app told us that the wait for Voyage of the Little Mermaid was less than 20 minutes, so we squeezed it in. This ride is similar to the Finding Nemo ride in Epcot, but the line that weaves you around caves with the sound of waves crashing and the smell of a salty sea in the air makes it worth the wait. There are screens hidden inside the rocks and a little cartoon crab that darts around through the different screens, and this is all before you're even on the ride.

Next, we went from under the sea to inside the mountain. My folks had ridden Seven Dwarfs Mine Train on Sunday while we were dragging ourselves to our room and said it was a blast. Dad especially liked the part when you got a view of all three castles before hurtling over the next hill. I was a bit disappointed that there weren't any of the mine games in the FP+ line, but seeing as the standby wait us was over 70 minutes, it was a good problem to have.

The coaster is so smooth you almost feel like you are floating as the forest, the mine, and scenes from *Snow White* rush by. When the ride slows inside the mine you are bombarded with colors of the different gems. The mine train winds through caves and then outside. You're moving so quickly that one minute you're inside trying to absorb all the colors and sounds and the next you're catapulted outside with trees, rocks, and glimpses of different castles whizzing by. My favorite part was the cabin at the end with Snow White and the Evil Queen as a witch. There was a bit of Disney magic sprinkled there which made it seem as if the witch is looking at you the entire time you are slowly rolling by. We all left the ride talking excitedly about our favorite parts and how the witch got a good look at each of us. We were feeling the Disney magic—a good thing because the next 30 minutes was anything but magical.

We began to make way from Fantasyland toward the Plaza Ice Cream Parlor on Main Street for our Wishes FastPass+. The park had seemed busy but not incredibly crowded, though now it felt like everyone was trying to move from Fantasyland to Main Street. Now I'm not super claustrophobic. An elevator full of spiders dangling from a bridge would be my personal hell, but big crowds don't affect me much. This crowd, however, would start to make the calmest person a bit crazy. It was the feeling that it was never going to end. It was wall-to-wall people, the majority of whom had decided to stop moving and just stake their spot for the show. Nothing was roped off, so no one was getting through. And people were trying to move in the opposite direction back toward Fantasyland as well. The poor cast members were trying to tell people they couldn't stop, but as soon as they turned their back, the crowd came to a standstill.

After 10 minutes of staring at various backs, death-gripping Oliver's hand so as not to lose him, and feeling the heat of a Florida day emanating from the black top, I started to feel my chest get heavy and it started to get harder to breath. I could tell I was starting to panic and told Joe I just want to get out of here. I don't care about the fireworks. Sam was in the same boat. Being short in a huge crowd is a huge disadvantage because there is no relief; you can see no end in sight. Just when it felt all hope was lost and we were going to spend the next hour stuck in a crowd of confused, angry, sweaty strangers I saw my dad waving his arms. We finally broke through the crowd and it was a miracle.

Finally, it came down to just a single cast member and his scanner standing in our way to some open space to watch the evening shows. The open space was reserved for FP+ guests, and it felt like entering an oasis. There was a huge grassy area, only a few people, fresh air, and a stunning view of the castle. It was like the heavens parted and the sun shown through. We could have hugged the older gentleman cast member who saved us from the ever-growing crowd. It was obvious this wasn't his first rodeo and he was happy to help us get away from the chaos.

After a quick headcount and comparing notes on how crazy that experience was, we staked out a nice big spot on the fake grass and took a breath. The only thing that would have made it perfect was a glass of Prosecco and a dessert plate. Everyone settled in, kicked off our shoes, got comfortable in various states of sitting, laying down, or leaning against each other, and caught the end of the Spectromagic parade.

I have seen Spectromagic a few times, but don't remember the music to be as redundant and grating on the nerves as it was this night. It wasn't as irritating as the hold music for a conference call, but pretty darn close. It became such a joke for our group we considered buying a CD of the music to torture one another. Yep, at the Emporium on Main Street you can get a CD from the Spectromagic parade. For money. The parade and its brightly colored lights and mind-numbing soundtrack made its way down Main Street and an announcement came about the upcoming Celebrate the Magic.

Disney knows how to do fireworks. It is like watching choreography, as Disney somehow gets the fireworks to dance. Everything is meticulously timed to the music and the colors almost seem brighter than other shows.

They even have shapes and, of course, the three fireworks timed to look just like Mickey always get a roar from the crowd. There are even incredibly bright fireworks that don't make a sound. How is that even possible? Austin and Dad were most excited for the fireworks, but for the rest of us it was all about seeing our Disney favorites take on new life projected onto Cinderella Castle.

Celebrate the Magic, also known as "the projections" in our house, are truly magical. It all starts with a very brave, petite young woman or man (boys can be Tink, too!) flying overhead as a glowing, sparkly Tinker Bell. Our group decided with absolutely no evidence that this Tinker Bell was a dude named Pedro. The folks next to us were confused when we all yelled "Hi, Pedro!" as Tinker Bell sailed by. Then, the park goes dark and the castle becomes the canvas for the Imagineers. The show follows a chronology of Disney film favorites, starting with Nate and Sam's favorite, *Steamboat Willie*. As time goes on, we see *Snow White* in Technicolor and the hand-drawn animation of *Sleeping Beauty*.

The castle continues to transform as the movies become more vibrant, featuring more color and computer-animation. The Imagineers take advantage of every square space of castle, having Belle & Beast dancing along the moat to the hundreds of colorful balloons from *Up* floating through the tallest tower. Ralph still wrecks the castle, you're taken into the glowing world of Rapunzel with the release of her birthday lanterns, and Walt appears to honor his favorite mouse. (The last performance of Celebrate the Magic was shown on November 3, 2016. It will be replaced by a show called Once Upon a Time.)

> **TIP!** Get the FP+ for Wishes so you can actually enjoy your Celebrate the Magic and Wishes experience. There are drawbacks of having a FastPass at the very end of your day, but it is worth it.

The park was packed, so Disney management decided to extend extra magic hours from 1–2 a.m. Austin, Nick, and I strongly considered rallying and going for it, just because we could. It was our second time at Magic Kingdom and we still hadn't taken on Pirates of the Caribbean, so while a few thousand people started heading to the front gates, we weaved our way across the hub and into Adventureland. It was a mistake.

The cast members at Pirates did not seem happy to be there, and our boat featured about 3 inches of water. Within our group of 11, we've probably been on these boats over 50 times and not once had any of us ever had this much water in the boat. There was more than one pair of ruined shoes. When informing the cast member he shrugged his shoulders and said, "okay," in a "what do you want me to do about it" way. This was the worst moment of the trip. Because of the extra pounds added by the small wading pool in our boat, it was sitting so low in the water that water was pouring in the sides. There was also a back up every few minutes and it felt more like bumper boats than the enjoyable ride we were all used to. We spent more time trying to stay dry and keep our shoes from being ruined than noticing the dog with keys, hairy legs, or even the auction in the town.

The crowds were still pretty big, so we headed up Main Street and stopped for a few treats at the Main Street Confectionery. While Oliver munched on a gigantic Mickey-shaped shortbread cookie that was buttery with a hint of saltiness, I inhaled a large, juicy strawberry covered in crunchy dark chocolate. The cheerful cast member at the cash register made up for her negligent colleague at Pirates of the Caribbean. She even took out a tray of the Halloween caramel apples so I could take a peek. There were Minnie witches with a purple witch's hat with an orange bow and Minnie's signature polka dot dress with purple sprinkles and orange frosting spots. Of course Mickey had to be in on the action with a Mickey pumpkin apple with the signature Mickey ears all in sparkling crunchy orange sprinkles with a chocolate frosting Jack-o-Lantern face. In other parks and at other shops you could find live out your Snow White fantasy with a green poisoned candy apple or celebrate with a Jack Skellington candy apple featuring white icing with a chocolate frosting Jack face. With our bellies full of Halloween treats, we left for our hotel. The park tried once more to give us a magical moment as we passed under the archway with a series of pumpkins spelling out "See ya real soon!"

CHAPTER TWENTY-ONE
The Kingdom of Bollywood and Everest

Day 5

We were starting to feel the wear and tear of the vacation. By the fifth day of a Disney vacation, you want to pull your feet off, sleep in, and walk less than 10 miles a day. But today was going to special because it meant Expedition Everest and our 10-year anniversary dinner at Jiko.

I woke up this morning craving bacon and eggs. Since most of us were still exhausted from the previous night, we decided to skip our 9 a.m. DINOSAUR FP+ and went in search of salty eggs and crispy bacon.

Why did our room have to be so far away? It was beautiful outside and after 10 minutes of walking inside and unsuccessfully trying three times to find a path outside, we gave up and headed back to the room to call for room service. By this time everyone was awake and my eggs had to wait while we banged on doors and took nine orders for breakfast. After waiting on hold and then finding out that room service would take 45 minutes, I gave up.

Being hungry brings out the evil in this stepmother, so Joe and I dragged Oliver with us to Animal Kingdom to go in search of food. It actually felt like Disney was determined to keep me from food. We headed to the Yak & Yeti quick service for some curry and ended up in the line with the confused cast member and the person who was unhappy with the menu offerings. After waiting for almost 25 minutes and then another 10 for our food, the moment was finally here. Food! Sadly, the curry was bland, Joe's salad was tasteless, but with enough ketchup, Oliver's fries, and a coke the size of my head, the hunger pains and bad mood started to subside.

> **TIP!** Plan at least one breakfast. This tip surprises me because one thing we learned in 2005 is to not schedule too many meals a day, but I honestly missed not having a normal (well, as normal as breakfast with nine people and Minnie Mouse wandering around can be) breakfast.

After meeting up with the other eight members of our group, we headed to Expedition Everest. The FastPass line was basically non-existent, so we were quickly packed in our cars. Our uneven number was not an issue for most Disney rides, but after extreme hunger and crappy curry, I was not thrilled about sitting next to a complete stranger for the ride I was looking forward to the most.

As you ride up to the top of Everest, you get this amazing view of the whole park. Look quickly because a second later you are hurtling in and out of the mountain, twisting and turning before coming up to a peak where the track has been destroyed by the mysterious Yeti. Just as you are about to exhale for the first time since boarding the ride, you are whipped backwards and your car is flying around twists and turns. (There was this part where we were going so fast in a circle backwards all I could do was scream and smile.) Then you are heading into a dark cave where the Yeti is supposed to appear. The ride speeds back to camp and everyone was talking about their favorite parts and those lucky folks who spotted the Yeti were bragging about it.

Our whole group was talking excitedly as we exited into a beautiful courtyard with the ride looming in the background. After some pics near a fountain in the courtyard with the white peaks of Everest behind us, Dad and I saw that the wait was only 30 minutes. "Should we go again?" I asked. It was unanimous. Everest was well worth a 30-minute wait. And it's an interesting wait. The line starts outside and winds through an area decked out with colorful Tibetan prayer flags, statues, and small courtyards that transport you to another world.

You then head inside to a detailed replica of a booking office for Everest Expeditions, complete with hiking gear, food supplies, and trip details. Also inside is a Yeti museum where the Imagineers had a blast telling the legend of the Yeti through reports, artifacts, and even videos. One of my favorite displays in the line is a bulletin board almost two layers deep of different notes, want ads, and messages about the Yeti. One is a list of other animals that you may have seen and mistaken as the Yeti. There are also fascinating posters advertising different services like Spice Traders and a vintage-looking ad for a product called Yeti Brand Muesli. After waiting about only 18 minutes, I told Joe we were riding together this time and he was helping me see the Yeti. Joe loves a good roller coaster. He loves to yell and laughs the whole time. It was much more enjoyable to yell along with him. I still couldn't see that darn Yeti, even with Joe's help, we but did get a great picture of the two of us with eyes wide open and screaming.

As we trekked around Asia, we came across a group of Bollywood dancers. Bollywood dancing is a blast, so it didn't take much convincing from the cast members to get me out there. I didn't have any luck convincing

Austin and Oliver to join me, but soon Annie, Sam, Nate, Nick, Joe, and I were all in on the action.

The music was upbeat and the dance involved a lot of bouncing and arm movements. My favorite is the one where you turn your body one way with both hands toward the ground and twist at the wrists, then switch with both hands up over your head. I've heard it's called the twisting the light bulb. Dad filmed the whole thing and we all got to relive our Bollywood moment of fame when it appeared on the DVD at Christmas.

"Can we see the tigers this time?" Oliver asked as we headed out of Asia. To the Maharaja Jungle Trek we went. Unfortunately, the tigers were sleepy and inactive. The theming in this attraction is amazing. It's as if you have wandered into the ruins of an ancient Asian city that has been taken over by the animals. We entered an area where a group of gazelle (or maybe it was deer) were running from a group of large horned cows that were coming through the grass very slowly.

Next, because it's one of Nate's favorite, we took in It's Tough to Be a Bug. As you exit the theater at the end of show, check out the tree and the view. There are great spots for pictures where the animals carved into the tree are quite pronounced. Pictures in front of the tree can be pretty busy and this was a nice quiet space where you didn't have to rush. The big thing at the time was to have two people holding a picture frame a few feet in front of everyone else. The rest of the group gets into the frame and the result is a fun pic. Our frame was a zebra print with an Animal Kingdom logo on it.

Our next stop was the Kilimanjaro Safaris, which turned into It's a Small World all over again, as there was a jeep back-up that resulted in our sitting for about 5 minutes watching the elephants wander around. There was a baby elephant hiding by its mother and a few elephants cooling themselves by flinging water on their backs with their trunks.

> **TIP!** Get PhotoPass photographers to take your picture. They have all sorts of ideas, tricks, props, and even after-effects at their disposal. We have a great pic of my parents in the France pavilion with Food & Wine logos on wine barrels as a frame. One favorite shot is of all of us in a half circle with our MagicBands in front of Tower of Terror. The Disney photographers know where to have you stand and can suggest fun poses. They will also take photos with your phone or camera.

Stomachs were starting to growl and dinner wasn't until later, so it was time to visit Harambe Market for some tasty meats. This space is still fairly new and a bit off the beaten path, making it not very busy. But the food is delicious. We munched on a thin sausage fried in a curry batter. It was almost a foot long and every one of us looked ridiculous eating it. It was too tasty for any of us to care. The sausage was slightly spicy with a hint of sweetness from the curry batter. Think of a carnival corn dog, but one you could get in Mumbai. It came with a tomato and broccoli salad that had a touch of vinegar that was a nice contrast to the heaviness of the batter on the sausage. Maggie munched on the chicken skewers that were a bit blander than the curry dog, but juicy and perfectly cooked. Originally, it was just Maggie and I who had decided to eat, and then Nick and Austin got their hands on the curry sausage. Four curry sausages later everyone was sated enough to head to the DINOSAUR ride.

DINOSAUR and I have a history. There are multiple pictures hidden in our house of me looking absolutely terrified on this ride. This trip did not disappoint and I was happy because I was not alone in my terror, though I think Nick and Nate just looked scared to make me feel less awkward. Austin was sitting between me and Maggie, and I'm holding his arm leaning away from the huge red dinosaur that's scaring the crap out of us all. Austin is also leaning away and into Maggie. Oliver has his hands over his ears and Sam is scrunched up with a huge smile on her face. The best is that Annie was in the front row, Maggie in the second, and Joe in the third, and all three of them have the exact same smiling, open-mouthed, loving-being-scared look on their faces. After DINOSAUR, it was time to hike back to our room and get fancy for our Jiko dinner.

> **TIP!** Dining with Disney can be a chilly experience because of the air conditioning. Make sure you dress accordingly. Pashminas or lightweight scarves are perfect. They fold up tiny, can dress up any outfit, and come in handy on the plane, for dinners, and even in some ride queues. For signature dining like Jiko, there is a dress code of business casual, so no gym shorts. Most of the girls in our group wore cute sundresses. The younger guys had polo shirts and khaki shorts or pants. Joe, Nate, and my dad wore button-down shirts.

This was the first time Oliver, Nick, and Sam got to see Animal Kingdom Lodge, in particular Jambo House, the home of Jiko, and most of our group didn't remember it from the wedding dinner in 2005. The lobby is amazing. It's 6-story-tall ceiling makes you feel as if you've entered a luxury hotel in Africa. The furnishings in the lobby reminded us of an old 1920's home, so we took one of those super-serious family photos you would see from the turn of the last century.

Our host for the evening was a young South African man named Cornelius. He was quite happy to be able to practice his English on our big crowd. Cornelius had an amazing accent and Sam commented, "He is beautiful. I want to wrap him in a box."

Jiko is a gourmet restaurant with tastes of Africa on the menu and plating that is on par with fine dining experiences in New York or Chicago.

Walking into Jiko is a play on the senses. The smell of meat and spices fills the air. The restaurant has dark wood furniture, deep red walls, tiled columns, and white sculptures that seem as if they are in flight along the bright blue ceiling. We were lucky to have a long table in the beautifully lit wine room. This isn't a standard room for seating, so there were only 5–6 other tables. The backdrop of our dinner was an ornate wall featuring an African pattern that looked as if it was carved of wood. The cast members are knowledgeable about the food and drink offerings and even had an extensive gluten-free menu for Maggie.

It was a night for celebrating, so I started with a glass of something pink and bubbly. There were a number of delicious sounding appetizers and we made the difficult decision of having the African table and indugay tibs in brik. The African table is similar to the bread service at Sanaa and has a series of dips with kobz, poppy seed lavash, and a crowd favorite, house-made naan. If "indugay tibs in brik" sounds like a group of unknown words strung together, it was for us, too. It consists of a deep-fried pastry with fillings that change with the seasons.

In addition to interesting surroundings and authentic and new foods, ordering at Jiko is a source of fun. Many of the dishes were quite exotic so we were amused listening to Austin order lamb while trying to pronounce ciabatta, Nick politely requesting a Nigerian-spiced pork chop, and Oliver asking, "May I have the steak with ancient grains, please?" "Just how ancient are those grains, Oliver?" asked Nate. After munching on the appetizers we rested our bellies to prepare for the main course.

"This is fantastic," Oliver declared about his steak. Austin and Joe munched on lamb two ways with pumpkin seed dugga and toasted olive ciabatta. Nick was amazed that his pork shank with apple butter was so tender that it fell off the bone. Maggie and Dad copied Nick, ordering the pork shank. Nate and Sam decided to share the pork shank and the mac and cheese with chakalaka and sausage. Annie and I decided to do African tapas and shared the boar tenderloin, maize soup, and the lobster tail with Madagascar vanilla bean-poached butter. The lobster was perfectly cooked and the vanilla brought out the sweetness in the lobster meat. My favorite was the sweet maize soup with a dollop of red peppery creaminess from a harissa crème fraîche, meaty blue crab, and a burst of sweetness and freshness from roasted corn. We fought over the crunchy Dhania biscuit.

Throughout the meal Nate had been acting suspicious, spending a lot of time on his phone, and it looked as if he was making notes. Nate and Sam started dating right before our wedding, so were coming up on *their* 10-year anniversary. He had been taking Sam's hints about engagement, but told Sam, Joe, Annie, and I prior to the trip that he was not proposing at Disney. This made Nate's behavior even wackier, and I wondered if he had changed his mind. What came next was one of the best moments of the whole trip: Nate's best man toast.

When we were married back in 2005 Nate was the best man, but he was a bit too young to know how to give a toast. His speech now was well worth the 10-year wait. He had written it out and it touched everyone's hearts. It's personal so I won't include the whole thing, but he had the table tearing up (even Nick) when he told Joe that he is his role model. He got a lot of laughs when sharing that his friends thought I was hot. He talked about our wedding and how he saw Joe get teary-eyed during our vows, and it made him tear-up but that was when he knew was true love was. And finally, he got a big round of applause when toasting Dad and Trish.

At that moment, I felt like the luckiest woman in the world because not only was I married to my best friend, but we had built this beautiful, caring family, a family that overcame a lot of obstacles to be together. And of course to have my parents there was just the icing on top of a magical Disney vacation. I may be a stepmom, but I am the luckiest stepmom to have these three amazing kids that accepted me into their lives, loved their little brothers, and have played such a major role in making life interesting.

After drying our eyes we decided it was time for a little dolci. The dessert menu featured even more new vocabulary words and a few of us decided that malva pudding was not just a Jiko dessert, but was also a 1920's cabaret dancer. Sam decided that Malva would have a deep throaty voice and catch-phrases like, "Come here, gents." The actual malva pudding was a fancy crème with cherries, crunchy toasted meringue, and a brandied cherry ice cream that added a brightness to balance the tartness from the cher-ries. Another favorite was the pot de crème, which is kind of like a crème brulee without the crunchy top. It was flavored with chocolate and Kenyan coffee, and topped with an almond crème, some almond crunch, and a few tart raspberries. Annie went with the Valrhona chocolate mousse with a hazelnut daquiose cake with strawberries and basil. This was renamed the Nutella dessert as it was passed around the table. I'm a salty-with-my-sweet girl and went with the cheese plate. It paired quite nicely with the sweet strawberries from Annie and crunchy, lemony meringue from Malva.

CHAPTER TWENTY-TWO
Be Our Guest

Day 6

Most guidebooks will tell you to rush to the parks and be the first ones there to get maximum ride time before it gets busy. If you have a limited number of days, an aggressive touring schedule, or have more attractions on your list than FastPasses, this is absolutely the way to go. But, when you're traveling with teenagers and a group that is on a different time zone, early mornings can be tricky. You have a one-hour window for the FP+ and our first FastPass was scheduled for 10:50 a.m. However, our FastPass was followed by one of the most highly anticipated events of the trip: lunch at Be Our Guest.

With our extra time in the morning, we all had breakfast out on our huge balcony with the wildebeests and ostriches. I've mentioned it before, but it really is magical being on the savannah. It almost becomes surreal and its not until you're showing pictures later and people say, "Wait, they were right there? That giraffe was just at that tree that's like 50 feet from your balcony? You were so close you could actually hear the animals munching on the grass?" that you realize it wasn't normal. It was Disney. And the answer to all those questions is yes.

> **TIP!** Plan at least one day where you can sleep in or just lounge around your hotel in the morning. That one morning where everyone just hangs out may be the thing that gets you through the rest of the trip.

One huge benefit of staying on site is Disney transportation. I've heard mixed reviews from folks on having a car and driving to the parks vs. using the free Disney buses, boats, and monorails. Having taken the monorail and seeing how full the parking lot is and the huge line to get into the parks and then leaving with about 5,000 other cars is not my idea of a vacation. We are from Chicago and traffic is a fairly regular occurrence for us, so being able to let someone else do all the driving for a week is an important part of a vacation for us. Also, paying $25–30 dollars a day for a car that will just sit in a parking lot for the majority of your trip seems wasteful. For a 6-day trip that's over $300 of your vacation budget. That could be lunch at both Be Our Guest and Sanaa.

On the other hand, Disney transportation is not perfect. The buses can have lines, can be crowded, and it can take awhile to get from where you're resting your head to your desired park. Also, if you want to go from one resort to another, good luck. You have to take a bus from your resort to a park and then a bus or boat or monorail from the park to the other resort. Depending on lines and timing, that can take well over an hour. With apps like Uber, getting a car is easy and can be cheap. But for us, between the monorail and buses we don't have many transportation complaints. And with a group of 11, we'd have to rent a church van to fit us all.

So, after bidding our furry friends farewell, we all made the long walk to the elevators with far less complaining and a sense of melancholy, as we knew it would be our last time.

Arriving at Magic Kingdom was bittersweet. For most of our trips I try to put Magic Kingdom as the last park we visit, and visit more than once. There is just something about Magic Kingdom. It is so quintessential Disney. You just feel Disney all around as you walk down Main Street with the brightly colored shops on either side, the smell of baked goodies and sweets filling the air, and Cinderella Castle towering over you at the end of the street.

We had taken a bit too much time relaxing and so we had to rush to make it to Peter Pan's Flight. This ride is a favorite of the group and is on our list of the required rides, like Small World, except it's far less grating on the nerves. There are not many cons of FastPasses, but one is that Disney has made waiting in line part of the experience. In the non-Fast-Pass line for Pater Pan, you are transported to London and the Darling's House. Guests can play games, view artwork from the film, and even see a replica of the nursery. Disney has worked hard to keep you out of line as much as possible, which really benefits them because then you have more time to spend shopping and eating, but if you do have to wait, it's going to be a magical wait. Add Peter Pan's Flight to Expedition Everest, Soarin', Seven Dwarfs Mine Train, Winnie the Pooh, and Haunted Mansion where waiting in line can be as fun as the ride itself.

After soaring over London in our pirate ships, it was finally time for Be Our Guest. I must stop for a moment and talk about the work that it took to get 11 people into this restaurant. It started with a phone call to Disney Dining and a lovely agent who said in her cheerful Disney voice, "Good luck." Her advice was to be persistent. This started my regular relationship with trying to book reservations online. Anytime I had a free moment or was on hold during another call, and every night before bed, I would be on the site trying to book.

Then one day in May it happened. I was able to get a lunch booking for 6 at 11:50 a.m. More than halfway there! How, I have no idea. With this renewed sense of hope I would try every day, often multiple times a day, to book for a party of 5, then 4, then 3, then 2, and finally 1. This went on for weeks with no luck, or only finding a reservation for 1 at 1:50 p.m. During the process it became clear that it may be impossible to get us all in for lunch. I spoke with Disney Dining agents and they told me Be Our Guest is the single hardest dining reservation to get in all of the parks. I wonder if its the hardest in all of Orlando.

Disney had been testing having breakfast at Be Our Guest and had not yet opened reservations for October. After reading that breakfast was officially staying, I was able to get a reservation for 3 for breakfast. At this point I had started splitting up our group trying to determine who would do breakfast and who would do lunch. As of July, I had a reservation for 1 at 11:05 a.m., 6 at 11:50 a.m., 1 at 12:30 p.m., and 1 at 1:50 p.m. Doesn't equal 11, right? Well, I also had a reservation for 3 at 9:50 a.m. and another for 1 at 8:45 a.m. Disney is smart and won't let you book multiple dining reservations under the same login, which meant that I had to keep creating new Disney profiles to book the reservations. During the months of June, July, August, and September, I would check at least once, sometimes multiple times a day, to try and get a reservation. As we got closer to our trip, Mom came over with news that Disney had pulled the plug on an outside reservation service that would book reservations for people and then cancel them all at the last minute. There had been a lot of complaints and Disney took action. Additional lunch reservations started to open up and I slowly was able to get more. It seemed lunch would be the winner! I finally was able to make reservations for all of us, though they were scattered from 11:35 a.m. to 12:10 p.m.

Now I tried to do the logical thing and contacted Disney to see if they could just merge them together. Nope. System doesn't allow that. They would have to cancel first and then try to re-book and there was no guarantee that the reservations wouldn't get snatched up. What the agent recommended was to arrive all at once and the cast members at the restaurant would likely let us go in together. She recommended that we go a few minutes before the first reservation. I had a note in my phone that was just the reservations and their confirmation numbers. After all that work, this place had better be amazing.

It was.

All eleven of us arrived a few minutes early for the first of our six reservations and just as the Disney Dining folks thought, the Be Our Guest cast members accommodated our entire group at the 11:35 time.

Right after check-in is where the true magic begins. It starts with a walk across a drawbridge where Beast's castle is peeking up over the rocks in the distance. The entrance into the castle features two wide stained-glass double doors. The foyer is carpeted in rich reds and gold and there is a stained glass window of Belle and non-Beast Beast to your left, framed by heavy velvet curtains.

After waiting in a short line with rows of chatty suits of armor (really listen to them, they have some interesting discussions), you enter a big room with touch-screen kiosks and cast members all around. On the screen is a picture menu; you just touch on the food, drink, and dessert you want, and then pay for it. If you don't have a MagicBand, you get a little rose that helps the cast members know where you are sitting; otherwise, your MagicBand is used. Whenever you have that MagicBand on, Disney knows exactly where you are. The waiters and waitresses, dressed in a version of the outfits of Lumière and Cogsworth, push large ornate carts with glass covers. It's all part of the theming that makes you feel as if you are at Versailles in the 18th century.

Be Our Guest has three dining rooms, the most popular being the Grand Ballroom which features pale yellow walls, an ornately painted ceiling, and large glass doors leading out onto a snowy night. If you have a large party, it's probably best to find a cast member to help you locate a large table. Another popular location is the West Wing, the smallest of the three dining rooms. It has dark ceilings and walls and the rose under a glass where you can sit and watch the petals fall. The coolest feature is a portrait of the Beast, pre-Beast. If you watch closely, you will see the portrait transform to the one in the movie with scratch marks.

Our group sat in the Rose Room, which was, sadly, not straight out of the movie, but has plush booths lining the walls. The highlight of the room is a large statue of Beast in his regal blue suit and Belle in her stunning yellow gown, dancing. It feels as if you are in a Beauty and the Beast-themed music box as Belle and Beast spin to the music. The walls are covered with tapestries featuring characters in famous moments from the film. A lovely thing about this room is there is less foot traffic as you try and enjoy your meal. Go and check out the magic in the other rooms, but don't discount the Rose Room as a worthwhile place for a relaxing meal.

Now, the food. We love French food and were very excited that Be Our Guest features French classics like croque monsieur and pork coq au vin style. I love that they didn't give in to "chicken nuggets and a hamburger" and stayed true to the venue's French roots. I have to admit I had an "evil stepmother" moment here. Disney is known for its generous portion sizes and Be Our Guest is no exception. I really wanted folks to share, especially when ordering the exact same meal, but alas, it didn't happen and a sad amount of French deliciousness was thrown away. The one drawback to ordering when hungry and ordering dessert at the same time as your meal is you don't know that you will be too full to move, let alone eat cake. So between the 11 of us we ordered pretty much every item on the menu.

Among the standouts were Joe's carved prime chuck roast beef sandwich, which in his words "was one of the best sandwiches I've ever had." It's served warm on crunchy French baguette, with tender, lightly seasoned roast beef, a spicy kick from the horseradish sour cream, and an added crunch from the peppery arugula. It comes with a side of thin, crispy pomme frites (French fries). Authentic French pomme frites are thin, crispy, and often dipped in some sort of rich, creamy sauce.

I stayed traditional with the croque monsieur, which is basically the French fancy version of a grilled cheese but instead of white bread and American cheese, you get hearty grain bread that soaks up the creamy béchamel sauce and salty Gruyere cheese. The bread is thick and keeps its crunch as all the ingredients mix together with the thick-sliced country ham. The croque monsieur is served with pommes frites and some of the fanciest ketchup ever in a beautiful ramekin. The meal comes on a crisp white plate, just like in a café in France.

After all the love for the pork at Jiko from Nick, Dad, and Maggie, Oliver and Austin both chose the braised pork with creamy mashed potatoes and French-style green beans. None of us like green bean all that much, but there's something about French style with butter and a sprinkle of almonds that make a veggie hater like me gobble them up. Maggie enjoyed the tuna Niçoise salad: lightly seared tuna, green beans, delicate fingerling potatoes, bell peppers, and a hard-boiled egg. After Jiko the previous evening, everyone's palate seemed more adventurous and open to new tastes.

The true highlight, and the best bite of the whole meal, was the master's cupcake featuring Lumière's gray stuff—you know, the one from the movie that's "delicious." This gray stuff was a light, fluffy frosting with a hint of dark cocoa piled high on a moist, rich chocolate cupcake. The gray stuff was topped with little baubles of silver, copper, and gold that added a delicious crunch contrast to the creamy stuff. My dessert was the most popular and eating something straight out of one of your favorite animated movies on what feels a bit like a movie set is surreal but definitely magical.

With our bellies full we decided to take it easy and ride Dumbo, another ride with a fun queue. After a short wait, you are handed a pager, which we thought would go off when it was our turn to ride. You're then directed to Dumbo's circus, a tent with a circus-themed playground inside. The playground was a lot of fun, and Austin, Oliver, and I had a rousing game of hide-and-seek. There are circus-themed bleachers scattered around the room, with dim lighting; if you have the ability to tune out the noise, it's a great place to close your eyes and rest your feet. The pager never went off and we learned after about 30 minutes of playing and confusion that you just hand it back in and get in the line to go out to the ride. Maybe when the park is busier, they use the pager system. The best part of the Dumbo ride was taking photos with an exact replica of the Dumbos you fly in on the ride. One of my favorite shots of the trip was the nine of us scattered around that Dumbo. Annie even climbed up the front and is dangling off.

After a spin on the teacups, we headed to the Many Adventures of Winnie the Pooh. Just the day before, after stalking the wait times on the My Disney Experience app, I had cancelled our Buzz Lightyear Space Ranger Spin FastPass and changed it to Pooh, a cute ride that transports you to famous scenes from the *Winnie the Pooh* books. It's simple like Peter Pan's Flight, but not quite as cool.

> **TIP!** When traveling with a large group, make everyone that is of a "make-able age" go to the bathroom when you stop. I don't have enough fingers and toes for the times we made a stop at the bathrooms when 2-3 people said they didn't have to go and right as the others are emerging, they decided they had to go. Maybe it was bladder envy? We must have spent several hours of our trip making bathroom breaks. I was a culprit as well, so am delivering this tip now a much wiser person after having spent almost 20 minutes at the bathrooms near Pirates of the Caribbean.

It was time for our first visit to Tomorrowland and Space Mountain, which is my vote for best roller coaster in all of Disney World. You can literally see nothing. You're speeding along and all of a sudden the bottom drops from beneath you as your hurtle down a huge hill, all in pitch black. This ride is incredible, and a Disney classic that incites no boredom. If you have anyone in your group who is afraid of the dark, it's probably best to pass on this one.

The next few hours were spent enjoying Tomorrowland, starting with Buzz Lightyear's Space Ranger Spin. At Monster's Inc. Laugh Floor we had a bit of magic when the cast member had Oliver magically open the doors by telling a funny joke. This is a cute show, similar to Turtle Time with Crush at Epcot, in that it involves some talented and witty improv comedians who perform the voices of the characters live during the show. The laugh floor is incredibly interactive. Give it a try and you may even be the guy who is "going to buy everyone churros after the show." Nick was able to get his Small World and Enchanted Tiki Room revenge by asking, "Can we go on the Stitch ride? I used to love this ride when I was a kid." Afterwards, even he admitted how bad it is. Seriously, skip Stitch's Great Escape. You'll thank me later

Then it was onto another classic, the Tomorrowland PeopleMover. The PeopleMover is an under-appreciated ride. It's cool to whiz around Tomorrowland above everyone's heads and you even get to hear guests screaming their heads off in Space Mountain with small glimpses of the roller-coaster track. This is another ride that is great for resting your feet or catching some quick shut-eye.

By this time, the park was starting to fill up for Mickey's Not-So-Scary Halloween Party. This event is popular because kids and adults are able to dress up and wear costumes in the park. Most days, adults are not allowed to wear costumes. During my wedding at Disney back in 2005, I inquired about pictures in the park and was told no because a woman in her wedding dress may confuse little girls and they will think she is a princess, and the only princesses in Disney are under the age of 26 and highly trained.

For most of the trip, we had avoided super-long lines or huge crowds (except for the nightmare before fireworks at Magic Kingdom). Leaving Magic Kingdom that night was not too pleasant. Most of the guests were all leaving at 7 p.m. because of the start of the Halloween party, so a few thousand people were all trying to board the monorail, boats, or buses at the exact same time. Our group was headed to the Polynesian for dinner at Kona Cafe and to watch the Hallowishes fireworks on the beach afterward.

After about a 10-minute wait in a huge crowd, we mushed ourselves onto the monorail and were off to the Polynesian. It's very cool to ride right up to a resort on the monorail. The Polynesian smells like vacation, has a great gift shop, and is busy—too busy for my taste. Kona Cafe is right in the lobby and is a bright, loud restaurant. After the intimacy and upscale experiences of Jiko and Be Our Guest, it was a bit jolting. Our table was right in the middle of the dining room, along the main walkway to the kitchen and to enter and exit the restaurant. We made the best of it, ordering sushi, Kona coffee-rubbed pork, and Oliver's favorite taste of the whole trip, a hot dog.

Our group was tired. There was a lot of discussion about whether to tough it out and see the fireworks. Funny enough, it was my parents who were the most up for another late night. I think they had been secretly running back to their hotel for naps or finding places to catch a few winks without us. It was decided we would forgo the fireworks and have a quiet evening of packing, watching *Aladdin*, and enjoying the last moments of vacation together.

> **TIP!** Is everyone on your souvenir list with you on your trip? Shopping is all part of the magic and few companies merchandise like Disney. So how can you get your fix if all the folks on your list are there buying for themselves? Have a Disney vacation award night. Figure out a trip-related award for each person and hit the park stores to find the prize.

It was now time to hop the monorail back to Magic Kingdom to catch the bus back to Kidani Village. On the monorail we were catching little glimpses of the Halloween party nighttime entertainment. Just as we made it to the bus station, the Mickey's Not-So-Scary Halloween fireworks, Hallowishes, started. My folks, Joe, and I were all taking our time walking back, savoring our last moments of vacation. The kids, however, saw that a bus to Kidani Village was there and went tearing off to catch it.

The four grown-ups decided to let them go and hung around to watch the fireworks, ignoring all the phone calls and texts of the kids freaking out that we missed the bus. These fireworks were very cool, with a lot of orange and purple. There was even a firework that we had never seen that started as a white circle, but then a strip changed to blue, then back to white across the whole circle. A Halloween-themed, color-changing firework. Only Disney.

CHAPTER TWENTY-THREE
The Disney Bubble Bursts

Day 7

The last day of a Disney vacation is always bittersweet. Your feet hurt so bad you think cutting them off may feel better. You could use a break from daily interactions with the general public. Your pants are fitting a bit tighter. Your wallet and credit cards need a few months (or years) to recover. You're ready to sleep in your own bed again and get a midnight snack that doesn't involve a 1/3 mile walk. Even with all that, the last day is always sad. Most of our group had moments when they were fighting back tears. All of us had waited 10 years (7 for Ollie) for this trip, the longest all of us had taken together. For me, that was almost the hardest part. Going from everyone together most of the time to all of us going back to our own lives. Thankfully, Christmas was coming soon and we would be together again soon, but the magic of the Disney bubble is a bit stronger than Santa, trees, cookies, and presents.

> **TIP!** Don't give up when something is lost. My dad lost his hat early in the trip on Big Thunder Mountain Railroad. Sam lost her Jack Skellington Mickey ears during the Buzz Lightyear ride. After searching high and low for another pair of ears to purchase, I ended up buying her a Queen of Hearts shoe ornament, but that did not fill the void. Sam was a woman on a mission. The morning of our last day she visited Guest Services at Magic Kingdom and lo and behold, she found both the hat and the ears. Her perseverance paid off and my dad was so happy to get his hat back. I think Sam and Dad built a special bond at that moment, and we even have a picture of the hat and ears on the day they were found.

CHAPTER TWENTY-FOUR
Not-So-Evil Stepmother Disney Secret #6

Five Keys to Making It Happily to the End of Your Disney Vacation

Key 1. Picture this: by the third day your feet hurt so bad you want to tear them off, you're tired of hearing complaints about lines, heat, or any number of other things not within your control, and you can't imagine enjoying one more minute let alone another 4 days of this.

There is no magical solution. Your feet are going to hurt. I so wish Disney would have a reflexology massage place in the China pavilion. It would challenge Anna and Elsa for popularity. Someone is going to crack and complain at some point and you will feel like all your hard work is not appreciated. But I can say you will make it through 4 more days. Not only that, it is likely within a week of getting home you will wish you were back there doing it all again. And there are some things you can do, starting with your feet. Bring a tennis ball or golf ball, throw it in a sock, and slowly run your feet along it. You can do this in the parks, but may get some strange looks, so I recommend you do it at your hotel after a long day. Pain medicine will help a little and if all else fails, cocktails. Epcot, the park that is biggest and hardest on the feet, may not have reflexology, but it does offer a wide array of tasty options to numb the pain.

Key 2. Schedule one day or at least a half day where you can do something again that you enjoyed the first time—maybe a ride, a show, somewhere to eat, or just another dip in the hotel pool.

Key 3. Make dining part of the experience. It's a chance to talk about what you did that day, and live it all over again. With restaurants featuring flavors from over 50 different countries, visiting Disney World is a chance to try new foods. Seeing Austin try butter chicken, naan, and African-spiced lamb and surprising even himself at how much he liked is a fun memory.

Key 4. Take a night off and hang in your room or by the pool. If a new Disney movie has just been released, watch it together as a family. If you are going for six or more days, this is really important, because it's easy to get Disney burnout and once it happens the rest of the trip can be affected. For some, Disney is a once-in-a-lifetime experience, and the need to ride every ride, see every show, and experience every single thing can result in exhaustion, short fuses, arguments, and bad memories. Not every moment of your trip will be perfect, but you will have many more magical memories if everyone has the chance to take a breath, recharge their batteries, and have unstructured time to relax. An afternoon at the pool may be all your group needs, but after doing this with every age range, I can tell you that sometimes it's the grown-ups who need the break the most.

Key 5. Be present. If you're the planner in the group, you'll find yourself focused more on checking the My Disney Experience app for the shortest wait time, making the next FP+/dining reservation, or making sure everyone else is where they're supposed to be and doing what they're supposed to be doing. You come home and realize you don't remember anything.

Stop and absorb the magic. For each day, schedule at least one thing where the organizer can just sit and hear about the trip. I suggest a dinner. Ask everyone what they liked about the day, what they want to see again. Not only do you get a few minutes to absorb, you'll learn how everyone is enjoying all those hours you spent on planning the trip. And hopefully this will also remind your group to thank you for all your hard work. Suddenly the daily phone calls to book Be Our Guest may feel a bit more worth it.

On the rides, be there. Take five pictures and then just sit back and enjoy. While riding Haunted Mansion on the most recent trip, I realized how different Disney can be when you remind yourself to stop and take it all in. Actually taste the ice cream, look around when walking from one attraction to the other, have a conversation, ask your group what they see that they think is magical. I'm no expert at this. I sit back now and have regrets on not really savoring moments when we were there. I had moments where I spent unnecessary time focused on what was happening next, where we needed to be, checking things off the list. Don't get me wrong, I have incredible memories and writing them down along the way for this book made me stop and remember more than on any previous trip. If there is any advice I hope you take, it's this: stop and savor the magic. Hug your kids, laugh with them, scream on a coaster, taste something new together—all of that will matter so much more than whether you made your Peter Pan FastPass.

CHAPTER TWENTY-FIVE
Not-So-Evil Stepmother
Disney Secret #7

. . . .

18 Ideas to Help Make the Magic Last

Disney withdrawal. It hits when you first get back, but then hits again a few months later. Solution? Talk about it. Don't ignore it, because it's awesome that your family had such a great time and that they miss it. Talk about what you miss. Figure out fun things you can do to relive moments. Create a video you can watch. Re-watch the planning DVD or create your own from pictures from the trip set to your favorite Disney songs. Give gifts that remind you of some of the magical memories. Have a DisneyBounding family meal. Pretend you are already planning your next trip and read a few blogs and share the latest Disney news with your family at dinner, a group text, or "like" something Disney related on Instagram or Facebook. There are many fun Disney games, both electronic and not, so play together, and of course, eat. With food you tap into your sense of taste, smell, and sight, and depending on what you are eating, touch and sound, too, which are huge in the memory-triggering department.

GIVE. When you're in the parks, buy gifts for upcoming events, like birthdays, anniversaries, or (if items are available) holidays—any gift-giving occasion will work. Bestowing your gift upon its lucky recipient will bring back Disney memories for both of you. Even if you're not in the parks, you can still make this work, through the Disney Store, Shutterfly, or any venue that carries Disney merchandise.

- Everyone in our group got in the act for the Christmas holiday and purchased Disney wrapping paper. Any gift that was Disney-themed featured this paper. Within our group of 11, the gifts were wrapped at three different households, but we all did the same thing.

- Disney knows that a picture is worth a thousand magical memories, and PhotoPass photographers are popping up everywhere. A fun post-trip activity is creating a photo book. PhotoPass photos can be quite pricey, so I purchase a photo book as a way to get many photos without the high price tag. Just going through and choosing and then deciding upon the layout is an interesting way to relive some moments, especially the ride photos.

- I also used our PhotoPass photos to create an Epcot mug for Maggie; a Phineas & Ferb mug for Oliver; Christmas ornaments for my parents, Nate, and Sam; a keychain for Austin (that he surprisingly uses); and magnets of their visit with Tigger for Annie and Nick.

- Through the wonderful world of smart phones, Joe and I used photos and Shutterfly to do a Frozen notebook for Maggie, playing cards for my mom and dad, and our Shutterfly favorite, a double-sided pillow for Annie that featured her with Tigger from 2005 on one side and 10 years later in 2015 when she found Tigger all on her own.

- Disneystore.com and now the Disney Parks app let you find the souvenir you missed while in the parks. Through these sites we found Oliver a Star Wars hoodie and Star Wars ugly Christmas sweater PJs. When he opened these on Christmas, Annie, Nick, and Nate were all on the app to see if they could get them in their size. We found my dad a cool shirt featuring a series of vintage tickets to the parks. The best was when we ordered a Dr. Who shirt for Nate from the Disney Parks app and received not only the shirt but a thoughtful letter from the folks at the shop in the UK pavilion at Epcot about how much our business means to them and their hope that we enjoy the shirt that was packaged and sent from the shop Nate had visited just a few months earlier.

- My dad won the award for the best gift with a photo-montage DVD. It started with the standard Disney movie opening, but customized to say "Daab 10 Year Anniversary" in the Disney font. Each group of photos began with a famous Walt Disney quote. The music was perfectly timed, mostly Disney tunes, and he even worked in video clips of rides, the Frozen Sing-Along, the Bollywood-style dance act most of the family joined in on, and other memorable events from our trip. The best part was before-and-after photos of each kid from our 2005 and 2015 trips. It was a fun and moving way to see how much everyone has changed and grown.

DRESS UP. Wear those Disney clothes even when you aren't at Disney.

- Annie has a necklace and a cool black hoodie with the four park icons on the back in silver and glitter (Cinderella Castle, Tower of Terror,

Tree of Life, and Spaceship Earth), Nate has his Beatles sweatshirt from 2005, Austin has a Pirates of the Caribbean shirt, Joe has the button-down I bought for him in Hollywood Studios, Oliver wears the t-shirt from his 2013 trip with all the characters outside the castle, Mags has vintage character shirts.

And I have my cream-colored sweatshirt with a black outline of the four park icons and my princess designer shoe pants that I bought during the 2013 trip. Similar to the shoe ornaments that are in the parks now and featured in a whole series of my photos from the 2015 trip, the pants have a high-fashion shoe for Ariel, Aurora, Belle, Cinderella, Jasmine, Rapunzel, Snow White, and Tinker Bell. It's Disney princesses (and fairies), but for grown-ups. I always fear for the day that I will come home and Annie will have confiscated them!

PRETEND. Just because you aren't already planning your next Disney vacation doesn't mean you can't still pretend that you are.

Before each trip I always read Disney books and blogs to get excited and to get the latest on what is happening in the parks. Now I'm reading Disney books because I like them. Theme Park Press has over 160 (at last count) Disney and Disney-related books to pick from: themeparkpress.com.

The *Oh My Disney* blog is a much-needed bit of pixie dust when the afternoon lull rolls around at work.

When you're tired of reading books to plan your next Disney vacation, find Disney books to read for pleasure. There's fiction; autobiographies and biographies of Disney Imagineers, artists, and animators; and even a book about Disney marketing and synergy written by a retired Disney executive. The business geek in me just exploded with glee!

PLAY. The best part of a Disney vacation is that you get to be a kid again. As Austin said to me, "You know how they say it's the place dreams come true and you can be a kid again, I love Disney because I feel like I can be a kid again." Bring some of that childlike wonder and enjoyment with you.

Watch Disney movies and talk about what you saw from the movies at the parks or what they reminded you of.

Play Disney board games like Beat the Parents, Phineas & Ferb 104 Days of Summer, or Disney trivia.

Reread journals and talk about what everyone remembers from different days.

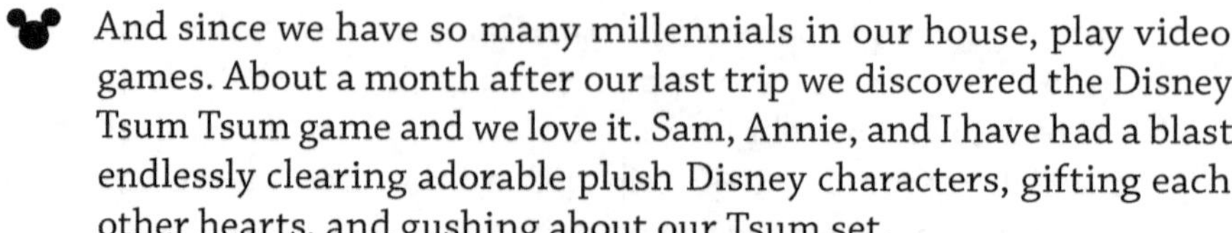 And since we have so many millennials in our house, play video games. About a month after our last trip we discovered the Disney Tsum Tsum game and we love it. Sam, Annie, and I have had a blast endlessly clearing adorable plush Disney characters, gifting each other hearts, and gushing about our Tsum set.

EAT. One of the best ways to trigger memories is smell and taste.

You can bring the tastes of Disney home with you through Disney cookbooks, the thousands of recipes online, or even ordering treats through the Disney Parks app. If you are like my mom, Joe, or Sam, toss aside recipes and create your own spin on some of your favorites.

At your next family meal have a souvenir that will trigger memories of one of your meals, like a copy of the *Beauty and the Beast* DVD for Be Our Guest or a toy convertible for Sci-Fi Dine-In Theater.

Get crafty and creative. Find a blank white paper tablecloth and a set of markers. Write the names of the restaurants you visited on your trip. Have each member of your family jot down a name with a new food they tried. Do a few fill in the blanks. For example: I miss eating at [ ] from our Disney trip? Then have everyone else try to guess the answer. Encourage the artists in your family to draw the restaurants or their favorite dishes.

Acknowledgments

Whether you're holding this book in your hand or reading it by the glow of the Kindle app, thank you.

Thank you Walt Disney and all the cast members for creating a magical world that we can all go to escape everyday stress and just be kids again.

Big thanks to all of my friends and family who read drafts, listened to ideas, and weren't afraid to say which ideas were bad, and for telling me that writing a book is a big deal! Special thanks to Pam, my dad, and my husband for the edit and proofs.

Bob McLain was willing to take a chance on a first-time author and Disney lover, and for that I will always be grateful. His books help bring even more Disney magic into the world.

Sam, the creator of the cover art of this book, thank you for having so much talent and excitement for this book, and for our trip. We're so happy you're officially becoming part of the family.

Nick, thank you for not packing enough socks, and for your love of Small World.

Mom and Dad, thank you for braving not one but two Disney trips with our high-energy group. Mom, thank you for being the thrill-seeker grandma and encouraging me to write this book. Dad, thank you for the thousands of photos you took. You made telling this story possible.

And last, but certainly not least, my family. You are a constant source of laughter, inspiration, and love. This book and the magical experiences on these pages wouldn't have been possible without you.

Nate, thank you for always being a kid at heart, for being able to make everyone laugh, and for GIRAFFES!

Maggie, the author of the family, thank you for all the good advice and editing tips.

Annie, social media advisor and 2015 trip hairstylist, thank you for all of your patience with my millions of questions about Instagram.

Austin, thank you for telling me I could do it and for always amazing me with your kindness, especially when playing catch with three little kids from Scotland.

Oliver, thank you for all the pats on the shoulder and hugs when I wanted to give up, and for not being afraid to battle Darth Vader.

And last but not least, to my better half and best friend, Joe. Thank you for saying, "just stop editing and send the synopsis" or "yeah, for the fiftieth time, the book is good." 14 years later and hugging you is still the best part of the day.

About the Author

The Not-So-Evil Stepmother, aka Trisha Daab, is the proud mom/bonus mom of five incredible Disney-loving kids. This is her first book, but the food at Disney has inspired her to write a second.

See photos from the Not-So-Evil Stepmother's Disney Wedding, Disney at Christmas, the souvenirs we couldn't live without, and more Disney love by following Trisha on Instagram @notsoevil_disneystepmom. You can also follow her on Amazon or contact her via email: trisha.daab@gmail.com

More Books from Theme Park Press

Theme Park Press is the largest independent publisher of Disney, Disney-related, and general interest theme park books in the world, with over 100 new releases each year.

We're always looking for new talent.

For a complete catalog, including book descriptions and excerpts, please visit:

ThemeParkPress.com

themeparkpress.com/books/disney-till-youre-dizzy.htm

Disney Trivia Overload!

You know you can't get enough. You know you don't *want* to get enough. Binge on enough Disneyland secrets, fantastic facts, and behind-the-scenes whispers to fill a Buick. You really will come out dizzier than Donald in a clothes dryer. But without the anger...

Letter Perfect
Walt Disney World

For every letter of the alphabet, there's a corresponding attraction, show, restaurant, or event at Disney World. Nicole Newport takes you on a unique tour of the most magical place on earth, from A to Z, in a family-friendly guide of facts and fun.

themeparkpress.com/books/disney-magic.htm

Lions and Tigers and Cast Members

Armed with a freshly minted degree in anthropology, Arielle Tuan found her job prospects less than hoped for. Then she heard of the professional internships at Disney's Animal Kingdom for college graduates interested in conservation. Apply? Why not! And from there her adventure begins...

themeparkpress.com/books/arielle-animal-kingdom.htm

Spoil the Grandkids at Walt Disney World

Former Disneyland tour guide (class of 1969!) Andrea Keech's unique primer about planning an *indulgent* vacation with the grandkids at Walt Disney World is both travel guide and story book. Full of advice and anecdotes, it's the only Disney travel planner for grandparents, by a grandparent!

themeparkpress.com/books/indulgent-grandparent.htm

A Monkey Paw in the Magic Kingdom

When R.J. and Suzanne Ogren "remember the magic" of Walt Disney World, they're not remembering their trips to the most magical place on earth, they're remembering their jobs: character performer (Suzanne), audio-animatronic artist (R.J.). Come relive it with them!

themeparkpress.com/books/remembering-magic.htm

Oh, You Didn't Know?

Just when you think you *do* know everything there is to know about Walt Disney World, here comes Jim Korkis with a new book full of stuff you won't easily find anywhere else. From the theme parks and resorts to "beyond the berm", this is the Disney that Disney forgot.

themeparkpress.com/books/secret-stories-disney-world-2.htm